Bearing Fruit

The Lord's Garden
by Diana Kleyn

Books in the Series:

Vol. 1 — *Taking Root: Conversion Stories for Children*

Vol. 2 — *Bearing Fruit: Stories about Godliness for Children*

Bearing Fruit

Stories about Godliness for Children

The Lord's Garden, Volume 2

by
Diana Kleyn

REFORMATION HERITAGE BOOKS
Grand Rapids, Michigan

© 2007 by Diana Kleyn

Published by
Reformation Heritage Books
2965 Leonard St., NE
Grand Rapids, MI 49525
616-977-0599 / Fax 616-285-3246
e-mail: orders@heritagebooks.org
website: www.heritagebooks.org

ISBN 978-1-60178-023-2

For additional Reformed literature, both new and used, request a free book list from Reformation Heritage Books at the above address.

The Lord's Garden

The books in this series are collections of devotional stories written for children. The stories are based on true happenings, gleaned from a variety of sources, and rewritten for contemporary readers. Most are culled from books of the nineteenth century, including several by Richard Newton. Modern presentations of these stories were originally published in *The Banner of Sovereign Grace Truth* magazine, and are now arranged thematically for the purposes of these volumes. Each story accompanies a passage of Scripture, and is intended to illustrate that particular biblical truth. Some stories are shorter, some longer. However, all will capture the attention of children, and hopefully their hearts.

Contents

1	Bearing Fruit	1
2	A Student Artist Learns a Lesson	6
3	The Glass Factory	9
4	A Godly Woman	11
5	The Storm and Its Lessons	15
6	"Boy Wanted"	17
7	Johnny Christie	22
8	Always Tell the Truth	25
9	A Conductor Learns a Lesson	28
10	Be Ye Kind One to Another	32
11	A Painter's Life Saved	37
12	An Indian's Conscience	39
13	Polished Boots	41
14	A Little Girl's Question	44
15	Listening to Conscience	47
16	A Dying Testimony	49
17	Rob McGregor	53
18	Courage to Pray	62
19	Elizabeth	64
20	A Faithful Saying	70
21	My Daddy is the Driver	73
22	Words Fitly Spoken	75
23	A Picture of God	78
24	Afraid of Lying	85
25	The Patient Christian Sufferer	87
26	Holding Daddy's Hand	94
27	The Angels' Charge	96
28	Love Your Enemies	98

29	Buddy	100
30	A Christian Lady	112
31	Forgive us our Debts	115
32	Time Spent Wisely	117
33	Not Afraid	124
34	The Powder Mine	125
35	Shaped for Heaven	128
36	The Wounded Soldier's Return	130
37	Rock of Ages	134
38	Slander and Gossip	136
39	The Bird and the Butterfly	138
40	The Living God	140
41	Lying Worse than Stealing	141
42	An Apology	142
43	The Retired Businessman	144

— 1 —
Bearing Fruit

And he shall be like a tree planted by the rivers of water, that bringeth forth his fruit in his season; his leaf also shall not wither; and whatsoever he doeth shall prosper.
—Psalm 1:3

In the Bible, God uses many examples of things in our lives to help us understand more difficult things. God wants His Word to be clear and simple so that even children can understand it. In Psalm 1:3, God uses the picture of a tree that bears fruit as a way of showing us what a godly person is like. Just like trees and plants bear fruit, so must the Christian bear spiritual fruit. Some plants and trees are meant to have only branches or stems, and leaves, and no fruit. But there are others that produce fruit: apple trees, tomato plants, blueberry bushes, etc. The apostle Paul, in his letter to the Galatians, describes the fruit of the Holy Spirit: "But the fruit of the Spirit is love, joy, peace, longsuffering,[1] gentleness, goodness, faith, meekness, temperance"[2] (Galatians 5:22, 23a). Through the work of the Holy Spirit in

---

1. Patience
2. Self-control

a believer's heart, this person begins to produce the fruit of the Spirit. This means that a person shows by his lifestyle that he walks in the ways of the Lord. Like you can tell an apple tree because of the tasty apples it carries on its branches, Christians should be recognized by having a godly character.

Did the believer always produce this fruit? No, for by nature we are born in sin, and we produce the fruit of sin. Many people who read the Bible and attend church forget something of utmost importance: there can be no fruit without life. Fruit cannot grow on a dead tree; it's just not possible. In other words, we cannot bear good, spiritual fruit unless we have been made alive by the work of the Holy Spirit. How can we receive this gift of life? Just as God makes the grass, plants, and trees grow, He gives the gift of eternal life in the hearts of His people. In John 15, the Lord Jesus tells His disciples that He is the vine. He was alive from all eternity. Only in Christ can we live, too. That is why Jesus

Fruitfulness

explains, "I am the vine, ye are the branches. He that abideth in me, and I in him, the same bringeth forth much fruit: for without me ye can do nothing" (John 15:5). Picture a vine or a tree, healthy and strong. A farmer cuts a branch from another tree and carefully grafts this branch into the healthy tree. Then, with God's blessing, this branch will live and produce much fruit. But if the farmer cuts off the branch and does not graft it into a living tree or vine, the branch will die.

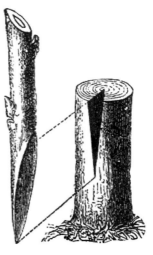

In the same way, a person cannot be saved unless he or she abides in Christ. Because we are completely dead in sin, we cannot make ourselves alive. The believer is alive only in the Lord Jesus Christ. Sin and Satan bring sin and destruction; God gives life and salvation because of the sacrifice for sin that Jesus made when He died and rose again. To be alive in Christ means that you have become aware of your dreadful danger and have fled for safety to the Lord Jesus; He has spared your life and given you the promise of eternal life in heaven with Him.

Does the believer change completely from someone who has brought forth evil fruit to someone who only produces good fruit? Sadly, no. As long as the Christian remains on this earth, he must battle against the sin that still remains in his heart. There are also many temptations in this world, and Satan is quick to try to get the Christian to stumble and fall. But because the Holy Spirit lives in the believer's heart and because the Lord Jesus has paid for the sins of every believer, there is the beginning of fruit-bearing, or holiness, in this life. The Christian often sins, but the Lord is faithful and will turn him back again and again. Each time, the believer must repent and confess his sins and be cleansed again.

Do you remember the story in the Old Testament about Aaron's rod? Read Numbers 16 and 17 with your parents. The Lord commanded the families of Israel to take rods, or branches, write their tribe's name on them, and lay them before God in the tabernacle. The rod of the man whom God had chosen would blossom. "And it came to pass, that on the morrow Moses went into the tabernacle of witness; and, behold, the rod of Aaron for the house of Levi was budded, and brought forth buds, and bloomed blossoms, and yielded almonds" (Numbers 17:8). God made a dead stick produce buds, blossoms, and fruit in one night!

This is a picture of what the Lord does in His children. In themselves, they are only like dead sticks, but when the Lord gives life, they bring forth fruit. Are you a plant growing in the Lord's garden? Are you a branch grafted into the true vine? Or are you still a dead stick? Has the Lord blessed you with new life? Have you come to realize that you are "dead in sins and trespasses" (Ephesians 2:1)? Have you already fled for safety to the Lord Jesus? Jesus warns us, "If a man abide not in me, he is cast forth as a branch, and is withered; and men gather them, and cast them into the fire, and they are burned" (John 15:6).

Dear children, it is important for us to see if we are firmly planted in Jesus Christ. One of the ways we do this is to look to see if the spiritual fruit of godliness is growing in our lives. So as you think about what God says about bearing fruit and read these stories about how God makes His people grow in godliness, pray to God and ask Him to be a good farmer and help produce these fruits in your life. Do not delay, but bend your knees now, and ask the Lord to save you. He will never turn away those who ask Him for new life in the name of the Lord Jesus Christ. May God be pleased to make you a fruitful plant in His garden!

—2—
A Student Artist Learns a Lesson

And we know that all things work together for good to them that love God, to them who are the called according to his purpose.
—Romans 8:28

Our heavenly Father deals with His people somewhat like the painter in this story dealt with his pupil. The student artist produced a beautiful picture which was admired by all. His young heart

A Student Artist Learns a Lesson

swelled with pride. He laid aside his palette and paints and sat daily before his easel, admiring the work of his hands.

One morning, however, he found, to his horror, that his canvas had been scraped clean. Gone was his masterpiece; only smudges of paint remained. He wept and shouted in anger and disappointment.

A little later, the master appeared in the studio. "What happened to my beautiful painting?" cried the student. "Who could have done such an awful thing?"

The master was silent a moment as he looked kindly into his pupil's tear-stained face. Then he said, "I did this."

"What?" the young man exclaimed. "Why? It was my best painting ever!"

"I have done this for your benefit," the older man explained. "That painting was ruining you."

"How? It was so good! I was so proud of it!" moaned the student.

"Exactly. In the admiration of your own talents, you were losing your love of the art itself. Now take up your pencil and your paints, and start again."

The young man sat stunned as he thought about his master's words. Shame rolled over him. How vain and proud he had been! As his anger disappeared, his heart was filled with thankfulness and admiration for his wise teacher. He dried his tears, picked up his pencil, and produced a masterpiece. If it were not for this harsh test, this young man's talents would have been hindered and stunted by his sinful pride. He never forgot this valuable lesson.

Children, remember this valuable lesson. Sometimes, like Jacob, we think that "all these things are against me!" (Genesis 42:36b). But if we are asking the Lord to bless us with eternal life, then He will work all things for our good. Sometimes things seem to go all wrong, and it seems that God has forgotten us, but if we are His children, then He will never forget us. We may not understand His ways while we live on this earth, but in heaven everything will make sense, and we will finally see that God's ways are best.

—3—
The Glass Factory

But he knoweth the way that I take: when he hath tried me, I shall come forth as gold.

—Job 23:10

George Whitefield once told this story. "When I was at Shields, I went into a glass factory. Watching carefully, I saw several masses of burning glass in various shapes and sizes. The workman took a piece of glass, and put it into a furnace. It was heated, and then removed. The man placed it into a second

furnace for a second heating; then a third. I questioned, 'Why do you put this piece of glass through so many fires?'"

"The workman answered, 'Sir, the first fire was not hot enough, nor the second. That is why we put it into the third furnace, which is the hottest. The intense heat of that furnace will make it pure and transparent!"

Just as the glass had to be heated to a very high temperature, so God's people must be "tried by fire" to burn out all their impurities. "Behold, I have refined thee, but not with silver; I have chosen thee in the furnace of affliction" (Isaiah 48:10).

—4—
A Godly Woman

By this shall all men know that ye are my disciples, if ye have love one to another.
—John 13:35

At least a hundred years ago, on one of the coldest days in February, a little boy stood peering into a shoe store window in New York City. He was barefoot and shivered in the cold. Just then, a lady rode up the street in a beautiful carriage, drawn by a fine black horse. She saw this little boy and noticed his bare feet and ragged clothes. Immediately, she ordered the driver of her carriage to stop. The richly dressed woman stepped down from the carriage and went quickly to the little boy.

"Little boy, why are you looking in that window?" she asked gently.

"I was asking God to give me a pair of shoes," answered the boy simply. "I don't have any boots.

They didn't fit me anymore, so my brother is wearing them now. I'm glad for him, though," he added quickly.

The lady smiled and took the little boy's cold hand. She led him into the store. If the salesclerks were shocked to see a wealthy woman holding a dirty, ragged little boy by the hand, they did not dare to show it. The owner of the shoe store hurried to be of assistance.

"Mrs. Wilson! It's good to see you! How may I help you?" he asked politely, as if it were a common thing for dirty little boys to be led into his store by wealthy patrons.

"Would you please send one of your clerks to buy a dozen pairs of warm woolen socks for this poor child?" she requested with a smile, handing him some coins.

"Certainly, ma'am! John, go and do as the lady asks!"

"Now," continued Mrs. Wilson, "would you please bring me a basin of water, some soap, and a couple of towels?"

"Yes, ma'am, I'll get them right away!" answered the shopkeeper.

When he brought the basin of warm water, Mrs. Wilson asked the overwhelmed little boy to sit in a chair. He looked at his ragged clothes, and then at the beautiful chair, and stammered, "I don't think I should sit there, ma'am."

Mrs. Wilson turned her gaze to a salesclerk standing nearby. Quickly, he placed a towel on the chair so it would not be soiled by the boy's dirty clothing. The little boy gingerly sat down. Then, to everyone's astonishment, Mrs. Wilson removed her gloves, knelt down, and washed the little boy's feet. Then she dried them with a towel. By the time she had finished, the clerk named John had returned with the socks. He handed them to the woman. She took one of the pairs and put them on the little boy's feet. Guessing what she would request next, the shopkeeper brought a pair of beautiful leather boots, which Mrs. Wilson put on the boy. She got up, smiled at the boy, and said, "I hope you feel better now."

Speechless, the boy looked at the socks and the boots, and then at the woman. He could think of nothing to say. Mrs. Wilson, however, did know what to say. "Do you have any brothers or sisters?" she asked. "You said you gave your old boots to your brother."

"Yes, ma'am, I have two brothers and two sisters. And a mother!" he added with pride.

Mrs. Wilson smiled, her eyes twinkling. "Would you like to go shopping for them? Should we keep it a surprise, or do you think they would like to come along?" She paused, thinking. "You know, I think they would like to come along. Would you please show me where you live? Then we can get acquainted and all go shopping together. What fun that will be!"

The astonished little boy looked up at her with tears in his eyes. In complete amazement, he asked, "Are you God's wife?"

Children, perhaps this makes you smile. We know that God does not have a wife. But do you understand why this boy asked this question? What did Jesus do for His disciples? He washed their feet. Whom did Jesus help and love? Weren't they often the poor and despised? The little boy actually gave Mrs. Wilson a beautiful compliment. Christians are called to be like Jesus, or Christ-like. The little boy noticed that God and the lady belonged together. Do you belong to God? Can others notice by your actions and your lifestyle that you belong to God?

—5—
The Storm and Its Lessons

The LORD is thy keeper.
—Psalm 121:5a

A severe thunderstorm was raging one night. Two little girls were tucked in their beds, but they were not sleeping. The flashing of the lightning and the rolling of the thunder frightened the children, and they hid their faces under their blankets. The girls' mother was still up. The children heard her singing one of her favorite Psalters:

> *O God, our help in ages past*
> *Our hope for years to come;*
> *Our shelter from the stormy blast,*
> *And our eternal home!*[1]

"Mommy!" cried one of the girls, "Aren't you afraid? How can you sing when the storm is so loud and scary?"

"My dear little girls," said their mother, kissing their cheeks, "How can I be afraid when I know that God is here? He takes care of us, and nothing can hurt us without His will. The lightning can do

---
1. Psalter 247:1 is based on Psalm 90.

nothing except what God wants it to do. So don't be afraid; just try to think about the fact that you are safe in God's care. He will care for you and me."

The girls' mother opened their Bible and read a few verses out of Psalm 91: "He that dwelleth in the secret place of the most High shall abide under the shadow of the Almighty. I will say of the LORD, He is my refuge and my fortress: my God; in him will I trust."

It wasn't long before the girls were sound asleep, comforted with the thought that God was watching over them.

—6—
"Boy Wanted"

This book of the law shall not depart out of thy mouth; but thou shalt meditate therein day and night, that thou mayest observe to do according to all that is written therein: for then thou shalt make thy way prosperous, and then thou shalt have good success.
— Joshua 1:8

Ben read the notice posted in the window of the nice-looking country hotel. "Boy wanted," it said.

"I wonder if I could get a job here," thought Ben. "I must do something to earn money, or how will poor Mother be able to live? I guess I'll go inside and ask about it."

So Ben went in. It was the first time he had ever been in a bar room. The place looked neat and clean, and there were no drunken men about. But the smell of the place was sickening, and Ben's heart sank at the thought of living in such a place.

The keeper of the house was a good-natured, pleasant-looking man. In payment for his services, he offered Ben a little room to sleep in as well as the tips he could make by holding the horses of travelers who stopped to get a drink, and by doing little jobs for them. In return for these privileges, he was to make himself generally useful about the place, and if the innkeeper was away, he was to pour drinks from the glittering bottles for anyone who could pay for them.

"Well, now," said the innkeeper, "you have heard what I want you to do. Are you ready to begin work?"

"Give me a few minutes to think it over," said Ben, "and I'll make up my mind."

"Well, you may think about it, but I can get plenty more boys if you don't like it," exclaimed the innkeeper gruffly. He was surprised that Ben did not take the job right away.

Ben said nothing more, but went out to the pump to get a drink of water. Then he sat down on a grassy bank to think the matter over. "What would Mother think of my working in a place like this? I think I would make a lot of money, but would she even want the money I made in this way? And what would God think of it? Doesn't it say somewhere in the Bible that a curse will be on the one who puts the bottle to his neighbor's lips? If I get used to selling liquor to others, it probably won't be long before I end up drinking myself. No, I just can't work in a place like this," decided Ben, and he returned to the tavern.

The innkeeper was standing on the porch. "Well, son, what do you think of my offer?"

"I cannot take it," answered Ben bravely. "I need work very badly, but I cannot do this sort of work. God would not like it, my mother would not like it, and I wouldn't like it myself. I am afraid that I might end up becoming an alcoholic. I'm sorry, sir, but I just cannot do it."

Ben walked away, leaving the innkeeper wondering why the boy would walk away from such a well-paying job. But there was another person who understood him very well. This gentleman had driven up in a carriage to inquire the way to the next town just as Ben had given his answer to the innkeeper. He was very pleased with Ben's courage and willingness to follow God in spite of the consequences. He quickly caught up to Ben and invited him to take a ride in his carriage since he wished to have a talk with him.

Ben climbed in, and the gentleman said, "My son, I honor you for refusing to work in a bar, and that is why you will be just the boy for me. I want a helper in my store whom I can trust, a boy who is faithful to God, to his mother, and to his own conscience. That is clearly the kind of boy you are, and the kind of boy I need."

The man offered Ben a good wage, and Ben went home to his mother that day as happy and thankful as a boy could be. Together they thanked the Lord for His protection, guidance, and care. "But whoso looketh into the perfect law of liberty, and continueth therein, he being not a forgetful hearer, but a doer of the work, this man shall be blessed in his deed" (James 1:25).

Ben had a difficult choice to make. Certainly, the offer of a good job was a real temptation, for his need for money was great. But this boy took the matter to the Lord, and the Lord richly rewarded him. We also face temptations. There are choices we must make, to sin or to flee from sin. Our hearts are naturally inclined to sin, so fleeing from sin is not something we can do on our own. We must turn to the Lord for help like Ben did in this little story. God will certainly help us if we ask Him to. Now, you must remember that there is not always a quick solution as in this story. Think of those in other countries who are tortured, imprisoned, and even killed for choosing God's ways. Is that because God doesn't bless them? No, their blessing is received in their hearts: they are filled with the love and peace that only comes from God. God's people here on earth certainly suffer, but through the Holy Spirit living in their hearts, they rejoice as they suffer for Christ's Name sake. They know that their lasting reward awaits them in heaven. "Blessed are they that do his commandments, that they may have right to the tree of life, and may enter in through the gates into the city" (Revelation 22:14). They know that one day they will be forever with the Lord, whom they love so dearly.

Do you love the Lord Jesus enough to suffer and even die for Him? Would you be willing to give up everything you own, and even be separated from those you love for the sake of Jesus? Ask the Holy Spirit to cleanse your heart from sin, and to fill you with His love.

—7—
Johnny Christie

Stand therefore, having your loins girt about with truth, and having on the breastplate of righteousness
— Ephesians 6:14

Two boys were in a classroom alone by themselves. One of them, who was named Johnny Christie, desired to walk in God's ways. The other boy, named Sandy Dawson, had no thought or care about God. Sandy had brought some fireworks, and he thought it would be great fun to set them off while the teacher was gone. When the teacher heard the bang and discovered the two boys in the classroom, he was angry with both of them. He first questioned Sandy.

"Sandy, did you set off those fireworks?" he asked.

Johnny Christie

"No, sir," answered Sandy.

"Johnny, was it you who did it then?" asked the teacher.

Johnny refused to say yes or no. So the teacher gave him a severe punishment for being, as he thought, both disobedient and stubborn.

At recess, when the two boys were together, Sandy Dawson asked Johnny, "Why didn't you just say you didn't do it?"

"Because there were only two of us in the room. If I said I didn't do it, it would have been obvious that one of us was lying."

"Then why didn't you say it?" persisted Sandy.

"Because you had already said you didn't do it, and I didn't want to accuse you of lying."

Sandy was stunned. He also felt guilty. Johnny had been willing to take the punishment for him in order to avoid accusing him of sin.

As soon as recess was over, Sandy went right up to the teacher and said, "Sir, I can't stand it that Johnny was punished instead of me. I told a lie. I was the one who set off the fireworks. Johnny had nothing to do with it. I'm sorry, sir," he said with tears in his eyes.

As the teacher listened to Sandy, he thought about his own guilt in punishing Johnny wrongfully. He had simply assumed that Johnny was guilty. His conscience smote him, and his eyes filled with tears too. He put his arm around Sandy's shoulder, and together they went to Johnny's desk. While the class listened in amazement, the teacher said, "Johnny, Sandy and I ask for your forgiveness. We were both wrong."

Everyone was very quiet. Johnny began to cry, for after all, it is hard to take a punishment you don't deserve. But he smiled through his tears at his teacher and at Sandy as he said, "Of course I forgive you!"

The entire class learned lessons that day that cannot be taught from books. They saw what it means to confess and to forgive. The children never forgot that day. Especially Sandy thought of that day as a turning point in his life. The teacher used the opportunity to teach the children about the punishment that Jesus took instead of His people. He urged the students not to ignore the Savior, but to flee to Him while they were still young.

"Remember now thy Creator in the days of thy youth, while the evil days come not, nor the years draw nigh, when thou shalt say, I have no pleasure in them" (Ecclesiastes 12:1).

—8—
Always Tell the Truth

Lie not one to another, seeing that ye have put off the old man with his deeds.   – Colossians 3:9

"Billy, don't go near that sand pile," warned his mother.

"But why not, Mommy? It looks like so much fun!" Billy was four years old and just learning that the world was bigger than his yard.

Billy's mother lifted him onto her lap and looked into his sparkling eyes. "Billy, if you go there, a bear will come and eat you up!"

The little boy looked frightened. "Bears?" he

echoed. "I'm scared of bears. I won't go near the sand, Mommy."

A few days later, Billy was playing with his friend Alexander who was a little older than he was.

"Billy, see that big sand pile over there? Let's go play in the sand!" suggested Alexander eagerly.

"No!" answered Billy firmly. "I'm scared of bears, aren't you?"

"What bears? There are no bears there! Who told you there were bears there?"

"My mommy told me," replied Billy. "And I'm not going near that sand, or a bear will eat me up!"

Alexander didn't quite believe Billy, but he saw that Billy was convinced about the bears. Just then, their pastor walked by and asked, "How are you boys doing? Not arguing, are you?"

"Not really," answered Alexander. "But Billy said there are bears in the sand pile and I don't believe him."

Billy's eyes filled with frustrated tears. "But my mommy told me there were bears there!"

The minister walked over to Billy and squatted down in front of him. "I'm sorry your mother said so, Billy, but the truth is, there are no bears there."

Billy began to cry, and ran home as fast as he could. "Mommy, Mommy!" he shouted. "Did you tell me a lie? Did you tell me that there are bears at the sand pile when there aren't any?"

Billy's mother wiped her hands on her apron

Always Tell the Truth

and sat down on a kitchen chair. At once she saw the sin of what she had done. She had told a lie. "I'm very sorry, Billy. I should not have told you a lie. I wanted you to stay away from that sand pile because I was worried that you might get buried in the sand. I told a lie to scare you away from the sand."

"But Mommy, you told me that it is a sin to tell a lie!" Billy looked into her face, his eyes revealing his confusion.

"Yes, dear, I know," she answered, tears springing to her eyes. "Shall we ask Jesus to forgive me? I pray that I will never tell another lie."

They knelt down to pray. Just as Billy's mother was about to begin, Billy stopped her. "Wait! Let me pray. Maybe you won't tell Him the truth."

This pierced her heart like a dagger. She realized that her little boy had lost his confidence in her truthfulness. Sin always brings grief and pain, sooner or later. Billy did learn to trust his mother again, and the pain was healed because of Jesus' love and forgiveness. But sometimes, sin's fruits are not so easily erased. Ask the Holy Spirit to make you clean and pure in the sight of God. Ask Jesus to forgive all your sins, and to keep you from sin.

—9—
A Conductor Learns a Lesson

Be kindly affectioned one to another with brotherly love; in honor preferring one another.
— Romans 12:10

A train was waiting at the station. The luggage was being loaded, people were hurrying back and forth with suitcases, and vendors were selling their wares. It was a busy place. A poorly dressed man made his way slowly to the train. He limped and walked with

A Conductor Learns a Lesson

a cane. The conductor slapped him roughly on the shoulder and said, "Hey, Lame-leg, hurry up or we'll leave without you!"

The man climbed aboard with some difficulty. No one helped him. The last of the luggage was loaded into the luggage car. "All aboard!" called the conductor.

The man took a seat near the window. After the train had been traveling for a few miles, the conductor came by to check the tickets. Noticing the poor man, he said rudely, "Hey, it's Lame-leg! Hand me your ticket!"

"I don't have a ticket," said the man very quietly.

"No ticket!" exclaimed the conductor. "Pick up your briefcase then, and we'll put you off the train at the next station. We don't give free rides to beggars."

"I would advise you not to be so rude, young man," replied the stranger.

The conductor muttered something under his breath and went on to check the tickets of the other passengers. As he stopped at a seat near the back of the train car, a gentleman, who had heard the conductor's conversation with the poorly dressed man, asked, "Do you know who that person is?"

"No, sir. I've never seen him before."

"Well, that's Mr. Warburton, the president of this railroad. I thought you might like to know."

The conductor's face turned pale. "Are you sure?" he stuttered. "He doesn't look like a rich man."

"Oh, yes, it's Mr. Warburton alright. I know him very well."

The conductor was horrified. He was ashamed of himself. How terribly rude he had been! Hardly able to concentrate on his work, he finished collecting the tickets, and then quickly made his way to Mr. Warburton. Emptying his pockets of the record-book, the tickets and money he had collected, he gave them to Mr. Warburton. "I'm quitting my job, sir."

The president picked up the things the conductor had laid on the seat. "Sit down, young man. I would like to talk with you."

The conductor sat down nervously. When Mr. Warburton turned to look at him, the conductor saw no trace of anger.

"My young friend," began the president, "I'm sorry to see you act in such a rude manner. You have acted very badly. If you were to act this way to all people you don't like, you would do a great deal of harm to the company. I could tell the Board of Directors about your behavior, but I won't. If I did, you would lose your job, and you would probably have a hard time finding another. In the future, remember to be gentle and polite to all you meet. You cannot judge a man by the coat he wears, and even the poorest ought to be treated with kindness. Take your things. I won't tell anyone what hap-

A Conductor Learns a Lesson

pened. If you improve your behavior, you may keep your job. Have a good day, young man."

Mr. Warburton stepped off the train, and the young conductor clumsily collected his papers. He had been taught a lesson that he would not soon forget. "Blessed are the meek," said Jesus in Matthew 5:5. "He that despiseth his neighbor sinneth: but he that hath mercy on the poor, happy is he" (Proverbs 14:21).

—10—
Be Ye Kind One to Another

We then that are strong ought to bear the infirmities of the weak, and not to please ourselves.
— Romans 15:1

"Stephen," called Mrs. Bennett as she stepped inside the door of her apartment. "I heard that Mr. Irving needs someone to work in his store. Why don't you go right now and talk to him about it?"

Stephen's face lit up at the prospect of getting a job. "That would be so nice, Mom, if we could find a way to make some more money. We sure need it!"

Mrs. Bennett nodded sadly. The death of her husband had made life very difficult for their family. She herself did what she could, sewing and washing clothes for other people. Stephen was the eldest of five children. The thought of sending him to beg in the streets of London frightened her. She had been asking the Lord to provide Stephen with a better way to earn money. Working for Mr. Irving seemed like a perfect job for her son.

She hummed as she made sure Stephen looked

Be Ye Kind One to Another

neat and clean before he set out. His clothes were well-mended; he had only one set of good clothes. His boots were a bit too small, and were worn through in the soles, but he was happy to have anything at all on his feet in this cold weather. A coat? He didn't even think of wishing for one. That would be a luxury!

With a goodbye wave to his mother and siblings, he set out, walking briskly to keep warm. He smiled, knowing his mother would gather the children around her and pray that the Lord would be with him. He added his own prayers with theirs. Five minutes later Stephen arrived at the store, but what he saw made his heart sink.

There, waiting on the sidewalk in front of the shop was a well-dressed boy. It looked as though he too wished to ask Mr. Irving about a job. Stephen sighed. Of course the nicely dressed boy would get the job. Who would hire a poor boy with patched clothes when a young man in nice clothes was available? Still, he had to try. Maybe Mr. Irving knew someone else who needed help.

Just then, a poor, shivering little girl crossed the street, and as she stepped onto the sidewalk in front of the two boys, she slipped on a patch of ice and fell in a puddle of melted snow. The well-dressed boy laughed rudely as the girl got up, water dripping from her thin, ragged clothes. She began to cry.

"My money! I had four nickels! Where are they?" she cried as she searched frantically for them in the slush with her bare hands.

Forgetting all about waiting for the shopkeeper, Stephen hurried over to the girl. "I'll help you. Don't cry," he said kindly.

Without hesitation, Stephen rolled up his sleeve, and felt around in the dirty puddle. He came up with three coins. "Sorry, little girl," he said, "but I think the other one is lost."

"Then I can't buy the bread," wailed the child, "and mama and the children will have no supper!"

Stephen knew what it was like to go hungry. He put his hand into his pocket and took out a few coins. He dropped the coins into his mittens. "Here, he said, holding them out to her. "These are for you. They're a bit big for you, but they'll keep your hands warm. If you carry your money in your mittens, you won't lose it so easily." He patted her shoulder like a big brother would do. "Go buy some supper for your family! Hurry or you'll catch cold!"

The little girl looked at Stephen in amazement. Then she dried her tears, whispered her thanks, and hurried on her way. Quickly, Stephen washed off his hands with some snow and dried them on his pants. He frowned when he noticed his damp, rumpled clothes. He would never get this job now! But he was glad he had helped the little girl. She was around his little sister's age, and he had vivid memories of her crying with hunger.

The well-dressed boy had watched all of this with a smirk. Now he laughed at Stephen. "Why did you even bother?" he scoffed.

Stephen looked up. He was about to answer when he noticed Mr. Irving. Oh no! Now he had no chance to go home and get cleaned up. But — Mr. Irving was smiling!

"What is your name, young man?"

The other boy gave his name, assuming that Mr. Irving would have nothing to do with Stephen.

"No, I mean the kind-hearted boy who helped someone in need," interrupted the shopkeeper.

"Oh! My name is Stephen Bennett, sir," replied Stephen. "I — I came to ask about the job."

"And you shall have it!" exclaimed Mr. Irving.

How surprised both boys were! The well-dressed boy left, grumbling about unfair treatment. Stephen could not keep the smile from his face. "Really, sir? My clothes...."

"Never mind your clothes right now, Stephen. Your actions tell me far more about yourself than your clothes do, and I am pleased with your actions. God tells us we must love Him above all and our neighbor as ourselves. I have seen you do the second part. I hope to learn that you live the first part also."

Stephen was prepared to make a sacrifice in order to help someone in need. In our days, you can't buy a supper anymore for four nickels, but certainly, there are still people who are needy. There are still many people who have less than others. There are children who have disabilities, or children who are shunned because of their looks or their accent, or because their clothes are not the latest fashions. Are you kind? Do you help others? Or are you selfish? Do you look down on others? Do you think yourself to be better than others? What does God want us to do? Remember who has given you all the blessings you enjoy. Ask the Lord to give you a new heart so that you can "love the Lord thy God with all thy heart, and with all thy soul, and with all thy strength, and with all thy mind; and thy neighbor as thyself" (Luke 10:29).

—11—
A Painter's Life Saved

For my thoughts are not your thoughts, neither are your ways my ways, saith the LORD. *For as the heavens are higher than the earth, so are my ways higher than your ways, and my thoughts than your thoughts.*
— Isaiah 55:8, 9

The story of Sir James Thornhill painting the inside of the cupola of St. Paul's Cathedral is probably well known to you. He and another painter stood on some scaffolding, since they were working high up. When Sir Thornhill had finished one of the com-

partments, he stepped back to get a full view of it. So intent was he on the painting that he forgot where he was. He did not hear the voice of the other painter, calling out to him of his danger. He backed nearer and nearer to the edge of the scaffold. Another step and he would fall to his death!

Thinking quickly, his

companion grabbed a wet paint brush and flung it against the wall, spattering the picture with unsightly blotches. Sir Thornhill flew forward in a rage. "What do you think you are doing!" he shouted.

Suddenly he realized what his friend had really done: he had saved his life! Knowing Sir Thornhill would rush forward to protect his painting, his friend had spared him from falling.

Just so, sometimes we get so absorbed with the world, and are unaware of our danger. We walk farther and farther away from God and from safety, and get nearer and nearer to perilous temptation. Then God, in His great mercy, "ruins our paintings" as it were; He seems to spoil something that we think is beautiful. We complain and murmur against His heavy hand. When the Holy Spirit shows us God's purpose and His love, however, we thank Him for keeping us from falling to our death. We realize that rather than ruining our wonderful life, God has been drawing us into His outstretched arms of mercy and grace. The very thing we thought was a disaster was actually meant for our salvation.

—12—
An Indian's Conscience

How much more shall the blood of Christ, who through the eternal Spirit offered himself without spot to God, purge your conscience from dead works to serve the living God?
— Hebrews 9:14

An old Indian once asked a man for some tobacco for his pipe. The man gave him a loose handful from his pocket. The next day the Indian came back and asked for the man. The owner of the store where the man worked asked him what he wanted.

"Sir," said the Indian, "I found a gold coin in the handful of tobacco he gave me. I want to give it back."

"Why don't you just keep it?" asked one of the customers.

The Indian turned to the customer. "I've got a good man and a bad man in here," he explained, pointing to his chest. "The good man says, 'It is not yours, give it back.' The bad man says, 'Never mind, you got it, and now it is yours.' The good man says, 'No, no! You may not keep it.' I did not know what to do, and I thought I would go to sleep and decide in the morning, but the good man and the bad man kept talking all night and troubled me. Now, when I bring the money back, I feel good, so I know the good man is right."

—13—
Polished Boots

Say not, I will do so to him as he hath done to me: I will render to the man according to his work.
— Proverbs 24:29

"I was in Egypt some years ago," wrote the Rev. J. Stuart Holden,[1] "and held some services for the soldiers. One evening I got into conversation with a sergeant in a Highland regiment. He was just as bright and shining for the Lord as it is possible for a saved soldier to be. I asked him, 'How were you brought to Christ?' This is his story:

"There is a private in this same company who

---

1. One of the scheduled passengers on the Titanic was J. Stuart Holden, eloquent preacher of St. Paul's Church in London. He had crossed the Atlantic many times to preach in the United States, often for Bible conferences. Less than 24 hours before the Titanic sailed, Holden's wife needed emergency surgery. The dilemma Holden faced was whether to fulfill his commitment to preach in the United States or to cancel his trip and remain with his wife. Trusting God's Word concerning his responsibility to his wife, he telegraphed the hosts of the conference that he would not be coming. Holden's Titanic ticket hung framed on his study wall for the rest of his life, as a testimony to God's faithfulness and guidance.

had been converted in Malta before the regiment continued on to Egypt. We gave that fellow an awful time. The devil had a willing accomplice in me, I confess, and I made that man's life a terrible burden for him. Of course, I did not realize then, as I know now, that I was in the devil's service as I persecuted that poor man. One wet and rainy night, he came in from his turn at sentry duty. He was very tired and very wet, but before getting into bed he got on his knees to pray. My boots were heavy with mud, and I hit him on one side of the head with my left boot, and on the other side of his head with the right one, but he simply continued with his prayers. The next morning I was shocked to find my boots beautifully cleaned and polished by my bedside! This was that private's reply to my wicked treatment of him, and it broke my hard heart. That day I repented and turned from sin and Satan to God."

Instead of becoming angry, this meek soldier had responded with compassion to his persecutor, and in so doing, won him to Christ. He had learned to recognize an opportunity to be Christ-like to his enemy. This is godly living: looking for opportunities not to hurt, but to love our neighbors. What do you think might have happened, had this soldier responded with angry words and actions? What might have happened if this young private had thrown back those dirty boots? There would certainly have been trouble. Solomon said, "He that is slow to anger is better than the mighty: and he that ruleth his spirit than he that taketh a city" (Proverbs 16:32). Often our actions speak louder than our words. Sometimes we may not have the opportunity to speak, but rather to keep silent, and to act in love. Jesus said, "Ye have heard that it hath been said, An eye for an eye, and a tooth for a tooth: but I say unto you, That ye resist not evil:[2] but whosoever shall smite thee on thy right cheek, turn to him the other also" (Matthew 5:38, 39).

---

[2]. This has also been translated, "do not resist an evil person," that is, don't fight back.

—14—
A Little Girl's Question

The father of the righteous shall greatly rejoice: and he that begetteth a wise child shall have joy of him.
— Proverbs 23:24

Mandy's mother was a dressmaker. If someone wanted a new dress, or a man wanted a new suit, he or she would go to the dressmaker's shop. The dressmaker would measure the person who needed the clothing and then sew the article of clothing for them. Sometimes, the dressmaker would go to the client's home if they requested this special service. One day, Mandy went with her mother to a wealthy woman's home in New York City. Mandy was five years old, a cheerful child, and a delight to everyone. This wealthy woman also liked Mandy at once.

"You have such a nice home," observed Mandy politely.

The lady smiled. "Would you like to see all the rooms in this house, Mandy?" she asked.

"Oh, yes! I would love that! My house doesn't have as many rooms in it as yours does!" exclaimed Mandy.

So they wandered from room to room, hand in

A Little Girl's Question

hand, chatting like they'd known each other always. Mandy exclaimed over everything she saw. One of the rooms had an exquisite carpet. "I think Jesus must come here very often," remarked Mandy. "You have such a nice house, and such beautiful carpet. It is like a palace. Jesus must come here very often. He comes to our house, and we don't have any carpet. Jesus comes here often, doesn't He?" questioned Mandy seriously.

The lady made no reply. She was surprised by the question and did not know how to answer.

"He comes here often, doesn't He?" repeated Mandy, tugging at the lady's hand.

The question had pierced the lady's conscience, and she answered honestly, "I'm afraid not, Mandy."

Mandy was very quiet after that. Soon afterward, she left with her mother. But God made use of Mandy's searching question. That evening the lady told her husband all about Mandy and the question she had asked. Mandy had assumed that such wealthy people would thank the Lord for His blessings, and that He was a welcome Guest in their home. The woman and her husband had to admit that they had taken their blessings for granted. They had not thanked God for anything, neither had they given Him their hearts. They were both convicted of the foolishness of living without the Lord. They began to read the Bible and went to church. The Holy Spirit blessed it to both of their hearts, and they became children of God. The Lord used the words of a little child to turn these people to Himself. "And a little child shall lead them," God's Word tells us in Isaiah 11:6b.

—15—
Listening to Conscience

And herein do I exercise myself, to have always a conscience void of offense toward God, and toward men.
— Acts 24:16

George Whitefield and a traveling companion stayed in an inn one night, as he toured the young country of America, preaching as he went. Mr. Whitefield and his friend were tired after a busy day in the service of God and were ready for a good night's sleep. They were very much bothered by the men in the next room who were drinking, gambling, and carrying on so loudly that Whitefield and his

friend couldn't sleep. Their cursing and foul language were easily heard through the thin walls. At last, Whitefield got out of bed and announced, "I will go and speak to them. They need to be warned against their sin."

His friend was worried. "They're drunk, and they will become angry with you. It's foolish! You might get hurt!"

But Whitefield wouldn't listen. He went to the men and spoke a few words of warning to them. No sooner had he closed the door to his room than the noise started up again.

"So, what did you gain by that?" impatiently asked his friend.

"A soft pillow," answered Whitefield with a smile, and he soon fell asleep.

What did Mr. Whitefield mean? He meant that he could now sleep in peace because his conscience was clear. He had told the men that their sin would lead to their destruction. He had urged them to turn to the Lord Jesus for salvation. The men did not listen, but Whitefield had proclaimed the gospel and now could sleep peacefully.

—16—
A Dying Testimony

That ye may with one mind and one mouth glorify God, even the Father of our Lord Jesus Christ.
— Romans 15:6

Quite some time ago, in Scotland, there lived a young man whom the Lord had saved. On this particular day, he was on his way to the hospital for an appointment with a doctor. He had sores on his tongue which just wouldn't heal. After a careful examination, the doctor discovered it was cancer. In a compassionate manner, the doctor explained to the young man and his parents, who had come with him, that the only hope of saving his life was to remove his tongue, in the hope that the cancer would be stopped.

"I want you to understand, John," explained the doctor, "that even if the surgery is successful, you will never be able to speak again." He paused, and then added, "We should do the surgery as soon as possible. How about today?"

John and his parents were shocked and saddened by the news the doctors gave them. They had come expecting some medicine from the doctor,

but instead they needed to stay for surgery. Imagine never being able to speak again!

The doctor and the nurses prepared for surgery. John was helped onto the operating table. Before his parents left the room, the doctor asked the young man if there was anything he wished to say before the operation began. For a moment a shadow crossed the face of the young man and tears rolled from the corners of his eyes as he considered that he would never again speak a word. Never again would he be able to praise, in word or song, his beloved Lord and Savior, who had done so much for him. But soon the tears stopped, and a smile lit up his face. A heavenly joy filled his heart as he began to sing this well-known hymn:

> *There is a fountain filled with blood,*
> *Drawn from Immanuel's veins;*

A Dying Testimony

And sinners, plunged beneath that flood,
Lose all their guilty stains.

With great feeling, he sang the second verse:

The dying thief rejoiced to see
That fountain in his day;
And there may I, though vile as he,
Wash all my sins away.

Before he reached the third verse, not an eye of those who stood around the bed was dry. His heart was in the song, his love to his precious Savior clearly evident.

Dear dying Lamb, Thy precious blood
Shall never lose its power;
Till all the ransomed Church of God
Be saved to sin no more.

E'er since, by faith, I saw the stream
Thy flowing wounds supply,
Redeeming love has been my theme,
And shall be till I die.

Then came the last verse, and everyone felt the presence of the Holy Spirit in the room, ministering to the young man.

When this poor lisping, stammering tongue
Lies silent in the grave,
Then in a nobler, sweeter song,
I'll sing Thy power to save.

John was then given the anesthesia, and the doctors performed the operation. But he never regained consciousness: he was taken to heaven to eternally praise and glorify his Redeemer.

Boys and girls, how do you use your tongues? Do you murmur and complain, lie, talk back to your parents and teachers, gossip, and slander? Or has the Christ that this young man knew and praised also made you a new creature? Is it your greatest joy to speak of the Lord Jesus? Do you long to praise Him perfectly, with your whole heart? Ask Him to give you a "new song," a new heart, which longs after Jesus. "And he hath put a new song in my mouth, even praise unto our God: many shall see it, and fear, and shall trust in the LORD" (Psalm 40:3).

—17—
Rob McGregor

The righteousness of the upright shall deliver them: but transgressors shall be taken in their own naughtiness.
— Proverbs 11:6

Three men stood leaning against some bales of wool in a large and spacious warehouse. One had a sheet of paper in his hand, on which he was trying to write with a huge pencil.

"No one will be able to read that, Tom," remarked one of the men. "Take the paper to Mr. Locker, and ask him to help you. He'll probably top it off with something from the company."

The third man, Ed Dufferin, agreed with this, so Tom slowly folded the paper and gave it to Ed, who then went in search of Mr. Locker. Mr. Locker was the foreman of that particular department of the business, and Ed found him in his office at the far end of the warehouse. The office was small. It had a narrow window, but because of the high walls of the buildings surrounding the warehouse, very little light was let in. Mr. Locker sat at his desk, a lamp lighting his work.

"What is it?" asked the foreman irritably. He was obviously not in a mood for interruptions.

"I just wanted to tell you, sir, that McGregor died this morning," answered Ed.

Mr. Locker looked up, his face full of concern. "Really? I'm sorry to hear it. We'll miss him here. He was a good, steady worker. It must have been rather sudden, but then I remember hearing he would not recover from his illness." He paused, then became businesslike again. "Well, we'll have to hire another hand immediately. Would you mind doing a little extra work until we find someone?"

"Sure, but I wasn't thinking about that," said Ed respectfully. "You see, he's left behind a wife and six children. We've been talking it over, and we'd like to write them a letter and send them some money. We'll do what we can among ourselves, but we don't have much to give, and we thought if the company would help a bit too, it would be a comfort to the poor widow."

"Ah, yes," responded Mr. Locker somewhat impatiently. "I'm busy now, but I'll ask the boss about it."

Ed remained standing with his hand on the doorway.

"Well, Dufferin," sighed Mr. Locker, "what else?"

"You see, sir, the eldest of the children is a teenaged boy. I remember you saying Dave Dicey wasn't enough, and that we'd better hire another boy to help. I thought perhaps you could hire Rob McGregor."

"To help Dave Dicey, I suppose?" remarked Mr. Locker sharply. "One young rascal like him is enough. He's always getting into trouble."

"Maybe he'll improve, sir," answered Ed mildly. "Anyhow, Rob's not like that. His father was a good Christian and brought up his children well."

"Hmm," pondered Mr. Locker. "I'll see about it."

Ed Dufferin gave the foreman directions to the McGregor home, and then left the office. He knew that even though Mr. Locker was sometimes brusque, his actions proved he was a kindhearted man, and trusted the McGregors would be provided for.

That same evening, Mr. Locker paid a visit at the home of the McGregor family. He found the widow so grieved by the loss of her husband that she was not able to think about how they would survive without him. In the corner of the kitchen sat an awkward looking boy holding a baby. His arms were too long for his sleeves and his legs too long for his pants. His face was not handsome although it was pleasant; there was an honesty and a kindness in his expression which softened the harsh features.

"Is that your son?" asked Mr. Locker.

"Yes, sir," answered Mrs. McGregor, "and there are five other children younger than Rob."

Turning to Rob, Mr. Locker asked, "Do you think you could do the work of an errand-boy at the warehouse?"

"I do not know the type of work you do, Mr. Locker, but I'll do my best," he answered with a hopeful look.

"I'll teach you about the work. Tell me, what did your father teach you?"

Rob's eyes filled with tears at the mention of his father, and he answered simply, "To fear God and to help my mother."

"Well, well," responded Mr. Locker gruffly, touched by his answer, "if you do that, you'll soon learn the rest. You may come to the warehouse at the beginning of next week."

Leaving a generous gift for the widow, Mr. Locker said goodnight. Mr. Locker understood that, although she hardly seemed to notice the money he laid on the table, she would indeed appreciate it later.

The men were glad to see McGregor's son among them, for he had been well liked, and his memory was respected. What most of the men did not really understand was that it was McGregor's deep, practical piety which had won their respect. He had lived what he believed, and his fellow workers came to love this quiet, steady man.

Dave Dicey was also very glad to have a new boy join the company. His reasons were far different than those of the others. He hoped to find a friend in Rob — a friend who would join him in his bad behavior, but Dave was soon disappointed. At first, Rob would quote what his father had told him when Dave urged him to be a partner in sin, but finding that Dave would only ridicule him, and that it did no good, he stopped trying to argue with Dave.

Dave, however, made another discovery which he thought was more pleasant than the first: Rob was very good-natured and never repeated what he learned about another person. As a result, Dave freely told Rob all about his pranks and offences, knowing that he was safe in his hands. Rob was often sorely tempted to tell someone, but the principles his father had taught him, and the Word of the God he loved and served, made him feel that he was bound to suffer anything rather than break a promise. Dave always managed to make him promise not to tell when he was going to confide to him any of his plots. Rob was wrong in making such promises; he did not understand that sometimes secrets must be shared with a responsible adult — that is, when a person or his property is in danger of harm or damage. But when Rob made these promises to keep Dave's secrets, he thought he should keep them.

Sin grows and worsens in the young if not restrained. Dave had become associated with a group of boys his own age. He wanted to do all the things they did, and go where they went. Since he did not have the money to join in all their parties and vices, Dave began to steal whatever he could. He would sell what he would steal, and use the money for alcohol and gambling. The workmen lost their tools, small pieces of machinery disappeared, articles of clothing vanished, and at last, a wallet belonging to Ed Dufferin was taken. There had been strong complaints which continually grew louder, but the theft of the wallet was the last straw. The men were determined to find the thief. Mr. Locker had heard rumors of Dave's bad behavior after hours, and he hinted to the men that it might be Dave.

In spite of Rob's good work habits and his cheerful character, he was not a favorite among the workmen. They thought of him as "slow." Since Rob was naturally shy, no one knew him very well. Dave, on the other hand, with his lively character and continual jokes, won their favor. Although Rob often made up Dave's work when he came in late, Dave was mean enough to make him the butt of his jokes.

Rob was hurt by this, and would often find a place among the bales of wool where he could cry a bit by himself and wonder why they were all so hard on him. But his father had told him that if he kept a conscience clear of offence to God and to man, he need never fear any harm. After pouring out his heart to God, he felt no bitterness to any of the men. He would come out from his hiding spot a little more shy, longing to get home so that he could read in his father's Bible, or wishing that it were Sunday again so that he could hear something to comfort and encourage him.

The men disagreed about who the thief could be. Some said that Rob was such a sneak, and so stingy (although Rob conscientiously brought all his earnings home to his mother) that he was most likely to be the culprit. Ed Dufferin and two others firmly maintained his innocence, believing it was Dave. One of the two boys, all were sure, was guilty.

Rob talked so little and listened so little to what others said, that he knew next to nothing of what had been going on around him. He was very surprised when he was called to answer to the workers. When he heard what he was suspected of, he looked at them in astonishment but answered not a word.

Ed said to him, "Surely, Rob, you are not guilty, are you?"

"You can't possibly think I did it!" he burst out, trembling with agitation.

"Well, this is the situation," another man explained. "It's between you and Dave, we're sure. We've heard that Dave runs with a bad crowd. Do you know anything about that?"

Rob only looked straight ahead and did not answer.

"Does he party at night?" asked one of the men.

"Can't you ask Dave?" returned Rob.

"Pretty sharp for the slow one," commented one of the men rudely. The contempt with which this was uttered, and the words the man spoke made an amazing change in Rob's face. The agitation left him and he stood firm and calm. Ed whispered to the man beside him, "They'll get nothing out of him!"

Ed Dufferin was right. They asked question after question. When they asked about his own whereabouts or activities, Rob gave ready, honest answers, but when they asked him about Dave, his lips were sealed.

Finally, tired of all the questions, Rob replied, "Do you know the iron gate?"

"Yes," answered the men, expecting some new information.

"Do you know Stockwell Street?"

"Yes."

"And do you know the street that leads out of that?"

"Yes."

"Do you know the big pump at the corner of that street?"

"Sure," they answered eagerly.

"Well, you may go and pump it as much as you like, but you will not pump any answers out of me!"

This unexpected finish, which so completely turned the tables on the men, produced a shout of laughter, which reached the ears of Mr. Locker.

When he heard what had happened, in addition to Rob's account of his whereabouts, he gave his verdict: "I hope you are satisfied, men, as I am. Rob is no more a thief than he is 'slow.' I have had my eye on him for a long time, but today's discovery of his integrity and his cleverness has gone farther still to convince me that he'll hold his head up through life and bring honor to his father's name and comfort to his mother."

Later, Mr. Locker drew out a confession from Dave. So, Rob did not have to "tell tales." The Lord took care of this honest young man. In the course of his life, Mr. Locker's prediction regarding Rob was abundantly fulfilled. "The integrity of the upright shall guide them: but the perverseness of transgressors shall destroy them" (Proverbs 11:3).

—18—
Courage to Pray

For whosoever shall be ashamed of me and of my words, of him shall the Son of man be ashamed, when he shall come in his own glory, and in his Father's and of the holy angels.
— Luke 9:26

Many years ago, a boy named Jamie got his first job on a wooden ship traveling from the River Nith[1] to Calcutta, India. He kept up his regular habit of kneeling for prayer before turning into his hammock for the night, not knowing he was doing anything unusual. An experienced sailor, Bob Shearer, who knew Jamie's parents, was watching the boy. He knew what to expect, and wanted to protect the boy from the rude comments of the other sailors. At Calcutta, some additional sailors boarded the ship, one of them a mean, foul-mouthed villain named George. Bob was especially concerned about how George would treat Jamie, for the hardened sailor seemed to have no morals whatsoever.

Sure enough, the homeward voyage had scarcely begun, when George, seeing young Jamie kneeling

---

1. The River Nith is located in southwest Scotland, between Sanquar and Thornhill.

Courage to Pray

by his hammock, swore and shouted, "Lookee here! A youngster at his prayers!" Laughing raucously, he threw a shoe with excellent aim at Jamie's head.

With lightning speed, Bob grabbed George, hauled him up on the deck, and thrashed him thoroughly. His lip and nose bleeding, George slunk away, muttering oaths under his breath.

Jamie had not thought his prayers would cause so much trouble. He was clearly shaken by George's reaction, and was afraid of the big man. The next night, Jamie decided to get into his hammock without kneeling. But Bob took Jamie by the heels and dragged him to his knees, saying, "Say your prayers like a man! Do you think I'm going to fight for a coward? Pray, or I'll need to thrash you next!"

This young boy was Sir James Anderson, commander of the Great Eastern,[2] who laid the first Atlantic cable. In this rough manner he learned a lesson he never forgot: that no boy or man should, under any circumstances, be ashamed of his colors, his conscience, or his God.

---

2. In the 1860's, the Great Eastern was the only ship large enough to carry the single length of cable needed to span the Atlantic. The Great Eastern laid the successful Atlantic cable of 1866 with James Anderson as her captain.

—19—
Elizabeth

But other fell into good ground, and brought forth fruit, some an hundredfold, some sixtyfold, some thirtyfold
— Matthew 13:8

In the summer of 1850, a minister made a preaching tour through part of the state of Virginia. Even then, Virginia was noted for its beauty, its fertile soil, and its rich mineral deposits. Sadly, it was also known for the lack of education and religion among the people who lived there.

Near the bank of a river, the circuit preacher met a group of men who were building a road. It was slow progress, and the men had put up their tents beside the river to house them during their time on the job. The men were friendly and invited the minister to spend the day with them. The minister used this opportunity to help out where he could, and to talk with the men about the Lord Jesus Christ. He handed each of them a tract or two, which the men politely accepted, although only a few of them could read.

Later in the day, a young woman, about twenty years old, came into the camp. The preacher introduced himself as a minister of the gospel, and told her that he had been invited to stay in the camp for the day. He asked the young woman about herself.

"My name is Elizabeth," she answered readily. "I live in the village down by the creek, which branches off this river. I'm here to collect the laundry for the men."

"Does your village have a church, Elizabeth?" asked the minister.

"Church?" Elizabeth looked at him incredulously. "We have a hard enough time building our cabins and barns, besides just keeping ourselves alive. Do you think we have extra time to build a church? No, we don't have any church."

"Doesn't anyone in your town meet together somewhere for worship?"

"No, we don't do that sort of thing."

"Have you never heard any preaching, Elizabeth?"

"Oh, I've been to a few big meetings when some religious people came through here, so yes, I've heard preaching five or six times," she frowned.

The preacher was amazed. "Have you only heard the gospel five or six times in your life?"

"Sometimes traveling preachers come through these parts of Virginia, and have tent meetings. I've been to five or six of those. I don't know what the gospel is, but I know there was preaching!"

Briefly, the minister explained the gospel to

Elizabeth, who listened politely, but made no response. "Have you ever heard this message before, Elizabeth?" he asked when he finished.

"No, I haven't," she shook her head.

"If you do not know the gospel, Elizabeth, then I am afraid you are not a Christian."

"No, sir, I'm not a Christian," the young woman asserted firmly. She was getting tired of all his questions.

"Don't you want to go to heaven when you die?" questioned the preacher.

"No, I don't want to go to heaven. I want to stay here."

"But you cannot stay here forever. One day you must die, and if you are not a true Christian, you will be sent to hell. Unless you are born again, you cannot go to heaven."

Elizabeth took a step back. She didn't want to hear his unpleasant message. "I have to go now. I don't want to talk about this anymore."

"Wait!" said the pastor. "I have something for you." He held out a tract. "This tells you about the Lord Jesus Christ who is willing to save sinners. Take this with you."

"I don't want it," answered Elizabeth.

"I'd like you to have it," persisted the minister. "It won't cost you anything. All I ask is that you read it."

"Read it!" Elizabeth exclaimed, thoroughly exasperated by this man who knew nothing about their hardships. "I can't read! I don't want your book!"

"Someone at home can read it to you. It may be used for your good," the pastor urged gently.

"Nobody at our house can read, so it's no use taking the book," she shrugged.

"Will any of your neighbors read it to you?" Elizabeth was annoyed at the man's determination.

Impatiently, Elizabeth replied, "None of our neighbors can read. I don't know anybody who can read, unless the boss over there can." She nodded toward the men working on the road. "Anyway, I've never heard anybody read."

"What about at the big meetings?" asked the preacher. "Didn't someone read from the Bible at those meetings?"

"No, nobody read out of any book. I'm sure I never saw a book. They preached and prayed, and sang some; but nobody read anything."

"Then I'm even more convinced that you should take this tract home with you, Elizabeth. It may be that the Lord will send some stranger to your house one day who will read it to you."

"Nobody ever comes by our cabin," she challenged. "We live far off the road in an out-of-the-way place." Then she sighed, as if she realized she could not escape the minister's perseverance. "I suppose your little book can't hurt me. I'll take it. Thank you."

She took the tract, slung the laundry bag over

her shoulder, and disappeared down the path into the woods. She was glad to get away from this persistent preacher.

Late that summer, a young man was on a journey through this same part of Virginia. To avoid the heat, he left the main road, and took a cooler, less-traveled path through the forest. The way was very lonely; he did not encounter a single person for more than eight miles. Finally, a cabin came into view. He dismounted and asked for some water for his horse and for himself. The family who lived in the cabin invited the young stranger inside, and kindly offered him something to eat and drink.

As he ate, he noticed a tract lying on a shelf near the table. Being a believer in the Lord Jesus Christ, he was delighted to see a tract in such a remote place. Pointing to it, he asked how they had

gotten the tract. The daughter answered, "A circuit preacher gave it to me a few months ago. He made me take it, and said that some traveler might come by one day and read it to us. Can you read, sir?"

Gladly, the young man read the tract to the whole family: father, mother, and six children. When he finished, the father asked him to read it once again. They were deeply interested, and talked about it for a long time. When the young man was ready to leave the next morning, they made him promise to visit on his return trip, so that he could read the tract to them again. This he did.

A friendship developed between the young man and this family, and with joy, the young man observed the Holy Spirit working in the lives of some of the family members. This young man was a relative of a member of the congregation of the same minister who gave Elizabeth the tract. How happy this faithful, persistent preacher was to hear that the tract he had left behind had been blessed by God. God's children scatter the seed with prayer and work, in faith and hope, and God will give the increase. "In the morning sow thy seed, and in the evening withhold not thine hand: for thou knowest not whether shall prosper, either this or that, or whether they both shall be alike good" (Eccl. 11:6).

—20—
A Faithful Saying

All nations whom thou hast made shall come and worship before thee, O Lord; and shall glorify thy name.
— Psalm 86:9

Here is a story about something that took place at a mission school in South Africa. It shows how even young children may be drawn to Jesus, and then may be used to draw others to Him. A man in Africa, who cared nothing for religion, was persuaded to send two of his children to the mission school. One of these children was an eight-year-old boy, and the other a girl of six. Since the station was some distance from their home, the children had to board at the house of the missionary. After they had been there some time, however, the father wanted the boy to help him in taking care of the cattle, so he went to the

A Faithful Saying

school to take him home. But the little boy had learned to love his teachers. He had also begun to love the lessons he was learning, and above all, he was feeling his heart drawn to Jesus and was beginning to love Him. He did not want to go home, and begged to stay. When his father asked the reason, he answered, "Because I can't learn anything like this at home."

"And what good things can a child like you learn here that you can't learn at home?" questioned the father impatiently.

"I have learned good things here, like this text: 'This is a faithful saying, and worthy of all acceptation, that Christ Jesus came into the world to save sinners; of whom I am chief' (1 Timothy 1:15). And, father, I have learned who Jesus Christ is. He is the Son of God. I have learned that we are all sinners, and that He saves sinners."

These words of his little boy had such an effect on the father that he went home alone and left his boy at the school. In a few weeks he came back to the school a changed man. That one verse had drawn his heart to Jesus, and his soul was saved. What about you? Is your soul saved? You hear many more texts than this man did. He heard only one text, and it was used for his salvation. What are you doing with all the texts you have learned? Do you treasure your Bible and read it often? Flee for salvation to the Lord Jesus Christ, the Savior of sinners.

Will you go lost, while those in far away countries who hear only bits and pieces of the gospel enter into the kingdom of heaven before you? Ask the Holy Spirit to cleanse your heart and to turn you from sin to God. That is the only way to true happiness and peace.

—21—
"My Daddy is the Driver"

Trust ye in the LORD for ever: for in the LORD JEHOVAH is everlasting strength.
— Isaiah 26:4

Many years ago, a man boarded the train as he always did on his way to work. The train was behind schedule, and was rushing along at an unusually high rate of speed in order to try to make up the time difference. The passengers were afraid that an accident might result, and many eyes reflected their fear. This man was also frightened and had visions of train wrecks in his mind's eye. Then he noticed

a little girl of about four years of age walking down the aisle. He had seen her before, and greeted her with a smile.

"Aren't you afraid to ride the train?" he asked.

"Sometimes I am afraid," admitted the little girl, "but not this morning!"

The man was surprised. "But everyone else is afraid this morning. Why aren't you afraid?"

"There's no danger," replied the little girl confidently, "because my Daddy is the driver today."

Her father was the engineer, and she had such complete confidence in his ability to protect her that she felt perfectly safe and happy.

If that little girl could have such confidence in her earthly father, how much more should we not trust the heavenly Father, who is "running the engine" of our lives? He orders and controls everything in heaven and on earth. If we are His child, then clouds and storms and darkness should not frighten us. Then He is our refuge and nothing can harm us while we are under His care.

—22—
Words Fitly Spoken

A word fitly spoken is like apples of gold in pictures of silver.
— Proverbs 25:11

Many years ago, Mr. Nelson was a deacon in a church in Central New York. He was a God-fearing man, and hardly a day passed that he did not speak to someone about their soul. In the same city lived Colonel Geoffrey, who took pleasure in ridiculing Christians and mocking the Bible. Mr. Nelson felt great concern for Colonel Geoffrey's soul, but he knew that anyone who had tried to speak to the colonel about God had made him terribly angry. The deacon, therefore, asked the Lord what he should do.

The Lord answered by providing him with an opportunity to visit Colonel Geoffrey on business. Mr. Nelson also talked with the colonel about eternity. He spoke earnestly about his need of a change of heart, and the necessity of trusting in Christ alone for salvation. The colonel, however, would not listen. He began to curse and to swear. He insulted the deacon, and scoffed at the words Mr. Nelson spoke. Mr. Nelson sat quietly as Colonel Geoffrey shouted at him.

The meekness of the deacon surprised the colonel. "Why don't you say anything?" he asked.

"Colonel," replied Mr. Nelson, "I knew what I had to expect from you, and before I left home, I prayed that God would give me the grace to bear it." His eyes filled with tears of compassion as he pleaded, "You are so unhappy! Won't you turn from your sin, and flee to Christ? How can you die as you are, and perish forever?"

Colonel Geoffrey was speechless. Overwhelmed at the love and meekness of this God-fearing deacon, he held his head in his hands, and groaned, "Oh, Mr. Nelson, what a poor miserable sinner I am!"

Mr. Nelson rejoiced inwardly. He read the Bible to Colonel Geoffrey. The very Book the colonel had mocked now became a precious source of hope to him. Mr. Nelson prayed with the colonel. The God whom this man had scorned as a figment of weak people's imaginations, now became real to him as a righteous, holy, just, but also merciful God who blots out the sins of His people through the atoning blood of Jesus Christ.

The colonel humbly came to the Lord Jesus Christ, confessing his sins. Faithful to His promise, the Holy Spirit washed his heart clean. He was born again. Formerly, Colonel Geoffrey had ridiculed God, His people, and Christianity. Now he spoke often of his loving Father, his gracious Redeemer, and the blessed Holy Spirit. His greatest joy was to see others begin a new life in Christ. The people he had so despised became his dearest friends, but Mr. Nelson always held a special place in the colonel's heart.

—23—
A Picture of God

For he hath made him to be sin for us, who knew no sin; that we might be made the righteousness of Christ.
— 2 Corinthians 5:21

It is a tragic fact that, to most people, God is a stranger. In Revelation 3:20, Jesus says, "Behold, I stand at the door, and knock: if any man hear my voice, and open the door, I will come in to him, and will sup with him, and he with me." How sad it is that when Jesus comes to people who should know Him, they do not hear His voice nor open the door. To know God really, truly, is eternal life. One of the best illustrations of who God is, is found in this simple story.

A minister lived in a New England town with his wife and one son who was about ten years old. One afternoon, the boy's teacher came to see the minister.

"Is your son sick?" asked the teacher.

"No," answered the father. "Why?"

"He was not at school today."

The father looked up in surprise. "Really?"

"Not yesterday either, nor the day before," stated the teacher.

"I had no idea," responded the minister thoughtfully.

"I thought he was sick and came to see how he was doing," explained the teacher.

"No, he's not sick," said the father slowly. "Thank you for stopping by."

The father sat in his chair, deep in thought. After a few minutes, he heard his son come in and went to meet him. One look at his father's face, and the boy knew his father had discovered his secret.

"Come with me, Phil."

Phil followed his father into the study and sat down nervously. His father shut the door and sat next to him.

"Phil, your teacher was here this afternoon. He tells me you were not at school today, or yesterday, or the day before that. Your mother and I believed you were at school. You allowed us to think that you were at school as you should have been. You don't know how disappointed I am. I have always trusted you. I could always say, 'I can trust my son, Phil.' And here you've been living a lie for three whole days. I feel very bad about this."

It was very hard for Phil to be spoken to in this quiet manner. Had his father shouted at him, it would not have been nearly so painful.

After a moment's pause, his father said, "Let's get down on our knees and pray."

Phil was becoming more and more uncomfortable. He didn't want to pray, but he got down on his knees beside his father. The father poured out his heart to God in prayer, and Phil knew as he listened to him, just how much he had hurt him. He felt as if he were looking in a mirror, and he didn't like what he saw.

When they got up from their knees, Phil noticed that his father's eyes were wet, like his own. The man laid his hand on the boy's shoulder and said, "My son, there is a law of life that where there is sin, there is suffering. You cannot separate those two things. Sin always brings grief and sorrow and suffering. Now," he continued, "you have done wrong. In this home, I am to be for you what God is in the world. God punishes sin. So we will do this: you will go to the attic. I will make a bed for you there on the floor. We will bring you your meals at the regular times. You are to stay in the attic for as long as you have been living a lie—three days and three nights."

Phil did not say a word. The attic! How dreadful! He had never been there in the dark, but during the day it was scary enough! Together Phil and his dad went up the stairs to the attic. Phil carried his school books. The father made up a bed on the floor. They dusted off a desk and found a chair.

A Picture of God 81

Phil's mother brought a couple of lamps and a Bible. Then they hugged and kissed Phil and left him alone in the attic.

Supper time came, and they brought Phil his plate. The mother and the father sat at the table in their cozy kitchen, but they could barely eat. They were thinking about Phil all alone in the attic. After a few bites, they gave up trying to eat. Mom wiped away her tears during the devotions. After supper, she cleaned up the dishes, and then joined her husband in the living room.

The father picked up the newspaper. He couldn't seem to make out the words, so he took off his glasses and carefully cleaned them. He put them on and tried again, and then realized he had been holding the newspaper upside down. With a sigh, he put the paper aside and tried to read a book, but he couldn't make sense of the words. He closed the book, leaned back in his chair, and began to pray silently.

The mother tried to do some mending, since she couldn't concentrate on her book. Her thread kept breaking, and she couldn't seem to get the stitches in the right place. She put aside the shirt she'd been working on, leaned back in his chair, and began to pray silently.

The clock struck nine, and then ten, but they made no move to get ready for bed. After a while, the mother said, "Aren't you going to bed, dear?"

"Not yet," answered the minister. "I think I'll stay up for a while. Why don't you just go to bed now?"

"No," replied the mother softly. "I think I'll wait a while too."

The clock struck eleven, and then twelve. "Could you please read a passage from the Bible and pray before we go to bed?" asked the mother.

Nodding, the father reached for his Bible. He opened it and read aloud. Then he prayed. Together they drew strength from God's Word and found comfort in bringing their son's needs to the throne of grace. Then they got up and went to bed, but not to sleep. Side by side, they lay quietly in the dark. They heard the clock strike one.

"Why aren't you asleep yet?" asked the mother.

"I can't stop thinking about Phil in the attic," replied the father.

"Me too."

The clock struck two, and the father sat up in bed. "I can't stand this anymore. I'm going upstairs with Phil."

He took his pillow and a blanket and went up the attic steps. Quietly he opened the door at the

A Picture of God

top of the stairs. He carefully made his way to the corner by the window. There lay Phil, wide awake, tears glistening in his eyes and trickling down his cheeks.

"Dad!" he cried. "I'm scared!" He reached out and put his arms around his father's neck, for they had always been the best of friends. Together they wept.

"I'll stay here with you," promised the father. He lay down beside the bed and at last they fell asleep.

The next night, when it was time for bed, the father said, "Good night, dear. I'm going upstairs with Phil." So he spent the second night beside his son on the floor in the attic.

The third night, the father said, "Good night, dear. I'm going upstairs again." This time he slept on the attic floor *instead* of his son. Phil could sleep in his own soft bed while his father willingly bore the punishment.

You will not be surprised to learn that Phil became a child of God. He never forgot the loving lesson his father taught him in those three long days and nights. He grew up to be a missionary in China, telling the people there the story of Jesus Christ, who suffered and died in the place of guilty sinners.

Don't you think this is a good illustration of who God is for His people? God did not take away the suffering caused by sin. Instead, He came down in the person of His Son and lay down alongside man for three days and three nights in the tomb. He suffered and died in the place of His people. That is God!

Now He comes and offers us life and salvation through Jesus Christ. He makes His people hate sin and long to be pure. To be loved by God, to commune with Him, to experience His forgiving grace, to be filled with joy and thanksgiving for Christ's sake — this is life eternal!

—24—
Afraid of Lying

A false witness shall not be unpunished, and he that speaketh lies shall not escape.
— Proverbs 19:5

One day a little boy named Kenny had been sent on an errand by his father. He had stopped several times to watch some boys playing in the park, to pet a beautiful dog, and to wander through the aisles of the general store on the street corner. At last he remembered that his father was waiting for the glue he had been sent to buy. He began to run as fast as he could to make up for lost time.

When he got near his home, one of his friends saw him and called out to him, "What's your hurry, Kenny?"

"I took so long getting my dad some glue, and now I'm afraid he'll be angry," Kenny answered when he caught his breath.

"Why don't you just say that the man in the store had to look a long time to find it," shrugged Kenny's friend.

"But he didn't have to look for it! It was right there on the shelf," said Kenny.

"So what? It would explain why you're late," reasoned his friend.

"But that would be a lie!" responded Kenny indignantly. "I don't tell lies! Even if I get the worst punishment my dad ever gave me, I won't tell a lie! My mom told me that lying leads to other sins. And the Bible tells me that no liars are allowed to enter heaven."

Kenny was right. Lying is a dreadful sin. David said in Psalm 51:6, "Thou desirest truth in the inward parts." Solomon said in Proverbs 12:22, "Lying lips are abomination to the LORD: but they that deal truly are his delight."

—25—
The Patient Christian Sufferer

That the trial of your faith, being much more precious than of gold that perisheth, though it be tried with fire, might be found unto praise and honor and glory at the appearing of Jesus Christ.

—1 Peter 1:7

This is the story of the life and death of a little boy named Willie McCourt. In 1884, when Willie was three years old and his sister Jenny was five, their father was tragically killed in an avalanche in Colorado. Mrs. McCourt was so upset and overwhelmed by this loss, that she had to be admitted to a mental institution and soon died. Jennie and Willie were taken in by some Christian women in Leadville, Colorado, the village in which they lived. These women wrote to an orphanage named "The Christian Home" in Iowa, asking them to take in these two children. So, in May of 1885, the children moved to the orphanage in Iowa.[1]

---

1. The Christian Home orphanage in Pottawattamie County, Council Bluffs, Iowa, was founded by the Rev. and Mrs. J. G.

Bearing Fruit

Jenny was a healthy child, but Willie had a deformity—severe curvature of the spine. During his first three years at the orphanage, Willie was able to play like the other children, although sometimes he was very rough and needed to be reprimanded. But often he would suddenly stop playing, doubled up with excruciating pain. Then he would have to be carried to his bed.

When Willie first came to the Christian Home,

Lemen in 1882, receiving children between the ages of 2 and 15. By 1883, there were about six children being cared for, but by 1886 that number grew to more than forty. By 1910, the home housed around fifty to one hundred children at any given time. For almost twenty years this couple devoted themselves to the care of the needy. Mrs. Lemen washed and scrubbed, baked and sewed, for the children in the Home as well as for her own children. At one time, typhoid developed in the institution and Mrs. Lemen assumed the responsibility for the care of seventeen of the sick children in addition to that of her own daughter who also contracted the disease. During the same years, Rev. Lemen carried the financial burdens of the growing and always needy institution. It was, indeed, a strenuous life and it is not surprising that these two people, whose faith, courage, and sacrifice made up the foundations of the Christian Home, died at a comparatively early age, Mrs. Lemen on September 10, 1902 and Reverend Lemen two years later. The home was then operated by the son of Rev. Lemen, H. R. Lemen and his wife who occupied a home near the orphanage. Florence Stephan, a niece of Rev. Lemen, took over operation in 1920. The facility is still in operation today, although it operates under the name of Children's Square U.S.A., continuing to do the good works started by the Lemen family. Source: www.webroots.com.

The Patient Christian Sufferer

he was not a nice boy. He was angry, rebellious, disobedient, and unpleasant. The workers in the home found it very difficult to punish him or correct him because he was so frail, so it seemed as if Willie would never become a child of God. After talking it over together, the workers decided to pray especially for Willie's conversion, and at the same time, earnestly try to lead him to Jesus Christ. God graciously blessed these efforts and answered the many prayers of the workers in the orphanage. Willie became very sorry for his sins and asked the Savior to make him clean. One happy day Willie exclaimed, "I love Jesus Christ so much, and I want very much to please

Him!" This made the workers very happy, and they continued in their prayers, asking God to keep Willie in His care and to perfect the good work begun by the Holy Spirit.

One of the workers later wrote this about Willie: "Glory be to the name of God, we have every reason to believe that this child, at that time six years old, was truly regenerated. We never witnessed a greater change in anyone. Before, he was selfish. From that blessed moment, he was ready to give up any candy or toy, no matter how highly treasured, to his playmates. Before, he was hard to get along with and disobedient. After that time, he was happy, obedient, and patient."

When he was seven years old, Willie had a terrible infection in his abdomen, and since that time he rarely left his bed. The best doctors in the area came to see Willie, but they all said there was nothing they could do to make him better. After this illness, Willie suffered every day of his life, but he never complained. He was a great blessing to all the children and the workers in the Home. When the doctors had to perform an operation with no medicine to numb the pain, he did not complain. And when the operation was finished, he would look up at them gratefully and say, "Thank you, doctors!" There were men in the room used to seeing people suffer, but not one of those doctors had a dry eye.

Willie suffered terribly. His little body was

The Patient Christian Sufferer

wrenched and twisted with pain. His back had sores which never healed. He underwent surgeries that would frighten the bravest man. It was impossible for him to lie on his back, so day and night he would lay face downward on a pile of pillows. His head was larger than it should have been, in comparison to the size of his body. His face was pale and suffering, but his eyes shone with love for his Savior. When asked how he was, his answer always was, "I'm alright," or, "I'm doing better." Even though it was plain to see that he was racked with pain in every limb, he rejoiced in his dear Savior.

Willie was a source of joy for everyone at the Home and for those who visited him. All who came into contact with him witnessed his great love for Jesus. He was always ready to speak of the Lord. Old and young, workers and ministers came to visit Willie. At Willie's bedside, God's people had their faith strengthened and were led nearer to the cross of Christ. He was greatly loved by all. Whatever was lovely in the Home was brought to his bedside. If there was a picture book, it was placed on his bedside table. If there was a canary, the cage was hung near his bed. If there were flowers, they bloomed in the window nearby. Everyone wanted to give their nicest gifts to Willie, to try to ease his suffering.

At last, after many years of intense suffering, God called Willie home, where there is no more pain, but only joy in the presence of the Lamb. Willie was conscious almost to his last breath. A short time before his death, he said, "I'll soon be with Jesus! I want to go to Jesus!" He died surrounded by the workers and the children of the Christian Home on Friday night, February 24, 1893, aged twelve years. They were very sad, yet rejoiced that Willie was now free of pain, and finally with Jesus Christ in heaven. The following Sunday his funeral took place. The casket was carried by six of the boys from the Christian Home, and it was followed by about one hundred workers and children. Four ministers spoke at the funeral service. All testified of the wonderful faith and intense suffering of little Willie.

The Lord was pleased to use Willie as an example for many others. Many children wrote letters to the Home after they read the story of Willie's life and death. One child wrote: "I have been afflicted for years, and have been too impatient. The account of what God has done for Willie has been blessed to my soul."

Another child wrote: "We were sad to hear of the death of dear Willie McCourt, for by his patience and Christ-like character he had endeared himself to us. He has heard Heaven say, 'Come, ye blessed of my Father,' and has entered into rest."

Still another child penned this letter: "My tears fell as I read that the life of dear Willie McCourt had been transferred from the clay tabernacle, which had been so full of suffering, to the Heavenly

The Patient Christian Sufferer 93

Home. For him all the agony of earth is finished, but the work which he began under God still goes on. The influence of his life will never be ended."

One of the workers wrote: "Little Willie has been a great burden. With him the Home workers have spent countless sleepless nights in the past five years. For hours at a time, one or another of them has held the patient little sufferer in their arms. Once every day and often many times a day, his sores, more painful than tongue can tell, have been dressed. But all this has been borne with joy, and our arms now ache for the little, helpless boy, while we rejoice that he is at rest in the arms of Jesus. Willie has been with us nearly eight years. He, with all his suffering and all the labor he cost us, was the light and joy of us all. He strengthened our faith and led us nearer to the cross. Praise God that He gave Willie into our care, and permitted us, in ministering to him, to minister to the Lord and Savior. His memory is a precious legacy. Little Willie, patient sufferer, Christian hero, farewell until that day when we meet in the Father's Home above!"

Another person wrote this: "What a sermon to the children is contained in Willie's conversion and his subsequent life. Jesus delights to save children. Tell the children of Willie; and by his life be encouraged as never before to labor to bring your little ones to Him who will take them in His arms of everlasting love."

—26—
Holding Daddy's Hand

Thou wilt keep him in perfect peace, whose mind is stayed on thee: because he trusteth in thee.
—Isaiah 26:3

Megan was a little girl, about six years old. At the end of the day, she loved to walk over to her father's office, which was only a few blocks away from her home.

"Come on, Daddy, let's go home," she would say.

"I'm so glad you came to walk with me," her father would say as he hugged Megan.

Today, Megan wanted to play a game. "Let's pretend I'm a blind girl, Daddy. I have to hold your hand, and you have to tell me what to watch out for."

So the bright blue eyes remained shut tight for the walk home, and Megan's daddy led her along. "Step up now, Megan," he would say, or, "Step down."

When they reached home, Megan excitedly told her mother what they had done. "Weren't you scared to walk around with your eyes shut?" she asked.

Holding Daddy's Hand

Megan beamed at her father and said, "Oh no, Mommy, I was holding Daddy's hand! I knew he would take good care of me!"

This is a beautiful illustration of what faith in God is and of the comfort it gives. God's children are perfectly safe when they put their hands in God's.

—27—
The Angels' Charge

The angel of the LORD encampeth round about them that fear him, and delivereth them.

—Psalm 34:7

Annie was a timid little girl. She did not like to be left alone in a dark room. One night after she had said her prayers, her mother helped her into bed. Giving her a good-night kiss, she was just leaving the room when she heard Annie say very softly, "Mommy?"

The mother went back to her little girl's bedside to see what she wanted. "The windows are making noises, and it sounds like someone's trying to get in," whimpered Annie.

"Well, I'll fix that," promised her mother. She put some wedges in the windows to stop their rattling. Then, sitting down by little Annie's bed, she said, "You're not afraid now, dear, when I am with you, are you?"

"No, Mommy. I don't mind the noise or feel afraid of anything when you're here with me."

"But, Annie, your heavenly Father can take much better care of you than I can. He is with you all the time. Let me teach you a beautiful verse from the Bible. I want you to remember it and repeat it

The Angels' Charge

to yourself whenever you feel afraid. This is the text: 'He shall give his angels charge over thee, to keep thee in all thy ways. They shall bear thee up in their hands, lest thou dash thy foot against a stone' (Ps. 91:11, 12). Say this verse until you know it and can remember it as long as you live."

Annie repeated the verses several times, and then she said, "Mommy, you can go downstairs now. I'm not afraid anymore."

So her mother kissed her and went downstairs. Little Annie went to sleep repeating the text she had just learned.

Are you ever afraid, children? You may always ask the Lord to protect you from sin and from danger. "For I, saith the LORD, will be unto her a wall of fire round about, and will be the glory in the midst of her" (Zechariah 2:5).

—28—
Love Your Enemies

But I say unto you, Love your enemies, bless them that curse you, do good to them that hate you, and pray for them which despitefully use you, and persecute you.
—Matthew 5:44

In one of the West India Islands, a man owned a servant who had been brought over from Africa. He had been taught the truths of the gospel by some missionaries, and by his honesty and good conduct had become so useful to his master that he made him overseer of his plantation. On one occasion, the owner of the plantation went to buy a number of additional servants and took this man with him to make his choices. After looking around for some time, the overseer fixed his attention on a poor, old, feeble man, and asked his master to buy that man. The master was very surprised and said the old man was useless, since he was too old to work much. But the overseer begged so hard, that at last the master gave in and bought the old man.

The overseer took the new slaves home and treated them very kindly. Especially the broken-down old African was treated tenderly. The overseer brought him to his own house and laid him on his own bed. Every day he prepared his food for him. When he was cold, he carried him into the sunshine, and when he was too warm, he placed him under the shade of the trees.

The master wondered why the overseer was treating this man with such kindness. "Is that old man your father, that you take so much interest in him?"

"No, master, he is not my father."

"Is he your brother, then, or some other relative?" asked the master.

"No, sir, he is no relation at all."

"Then why do you take such good care of this old man?"

"Master," replied the overseer, "he is my old enemy. He took me away from my home in Africa and sold me to the trader. But the Bible tells me to love my enemy.

"When he is hungry I must feed him, and when he is thirsty, I must give him drink. And so, I am only doing what my Bible tells me to do."

—29—
Buddy

We met Buddy on July 7, 2006, while having lunch in the dining room of the Missionary Guest House in Port Morisby. This is her story:

In one of the thatch-roofed houses in Ukarumpa, a village in the High Lands of Papua New Guinea (PNG), lived a little, black girl with a head full of frizzy, black curls.

In church

On Sundays, Buddy, for that was her name, went with her parents to the church close by. In the dry season, she would run ahead of her parents, making little detours as she went, but this time it was raining, and Buddy took shelter under her mother's umbrella, careful not to slip on the slithery, red-clay path. When they arrived at the small bamboo-and-thatch church building, Mama shook hands with the other ladies and then entered and sat down with her two little daughters on one of the rough wooden benches on the left, while her father sat with the men on the right side.

Buddy

The minister preached for a long time, and Buddy tried to remember what he said. The congregation sang many songs about Jesus, whose blood was spilled on the cross. At the end of the sermon, the minister told the people which texts to learn from their Bibles. This time, there were ten verses. But Buddy was a smart girl, and she loved to learn; she would make sure she knew her texts the next Sunday. While she was helping Mom in the garden on the mountain slope or doing the laundry in the river, she and her mother often repeated the texts.

Hungering for God

Buddy loved to go to school to learn and play with the other children. She was a privileged girl, for not all the children in PNG go to school, but *her* father was willing to pay the school fees. What a good father she had!

Yet, Buddy did not feel happy. Sure, she loved splashing in the river, or zipping down the mountain slope on a banana leaf with her friends; but she was not really happy. She knew many texts of the Bible by heart, and could even recite whole chapters, but that did not satisfy her. Her trouble was that she did not know God. She hungered for Him. At night, she knelt down on her mat in the corner of the hut and asked the Lord to show her who He was.

Learning to know her heart
However, the more Buddy prayed, the more she began to see that she was sinful. That frightened her: bad girls go to hell! The pastor in church often said you had to be good to go to heaven. But Buddy knew she was not good. When her mom told her to work in the garden, she obeyed, but she knew that in her heart she often disobeyed. When someone said something bad about her, she would get so very angry, and she knew that that was not right. "No, I am not good," Buddy decided.

Searching for God
As Buddy became older, she began to attend other churches. You should know that there are many churches in PNG—little groups of thirty or forty men, women, and children meet in their little prayer houses, or even just under their umbrellas in the open. Her father was not happy that Buddy no longer went to church with the family. He said, "Buddy, what you are doing is not good. Why don't you go to church with us? Why do you have to be so different?" He did not understand that his daughter had to find God!

All the while, however, Buddy kept praying for God to show Himself to her.

Deliverance
One Sunday in church, the minister said, "We are

born in sin and we can never make ourselves clean, no matter how hard we try. But this is the good message: 'The blood of Christ, his Son, cleanses us from all sin' (1 John 1:7)!" He wrote the words in large letters on the whiteboard. At that moment, a heavy load fell off Buddy's heart. For the first time in her life, she felt happy. God had given her faith and the blood of Jesus Christ, who died on the cross. Her sins were forgiven. God had made her clean!

Coming home, she read her Bible. It was so different now! The whole Bible went open for her. She drank in the words of salvation. A new desire was born in her heart. She wanted to serve the Lord who died for her. She told her father, "I want to work for the Lord. I want to make His Name known to other people! So many of our people don't know Him." "Oh, Buddy," her father replied. "Why do you have such strange ideas? Just work in the garden, sell your crop at the market, and you will be happy."

Working on the boat

But Buddy knew that the Lord was calling her. She found work on *The Logos*, a floating Christian library and bookstore that goes from island to island in the South Pacific Ocean. She had to find her own support for this work, which was not easy. But to use her own words: "The Lord provided bread and even butter every day."

Sometimes, however, Buddy's faith was not so strong. One day, she sat sobbing on the deck.

Another girl came to her and asked, "What's the matter, Buddy?" "Oh, my church won't support me!" Buddy complained. "They think it's great that I do this work, but they don't provide me with any assistance." "Oh, Buddy," the girl answered. "Don't we all experience difficulties? Think of what the Lord Jesus went through!"

At that moment, Buddy's heart melted. What unthankful thoughts she had had! As soon as she had a chance, she went to her church leaders and confessed with tears what unkind thoughts she had harbored about them. The leaders of the church were moved when they heard Buddy's confession; from that time on, they supported her.

Bible School

After some years on the boat, Buddy felt that the Lord was calling her to work among her own people in Ukarumpa. There are many Bible translators living in Ukarumpa Center, because a Wycliff Bible translation compound is situated near the Ukarumpa village where about two thousand people live and work. Still, many nationals are ignorant of the gospel and living in fear of the spirits of their ancestors. They think that Jesus Christ is a tall, Western man in flowing white robes who cannot possibly have anything to do with nationals. But how could Buddy help them? She herself was still so ignorant of Bible doctrines. Buddy prayed a lot about this matter. Then, a way was opened for her to attend Bible School. Again she had to find her own support, but the Lord provided wonderfully. Her parents' hearts were changed, and now they did all in their power to keep their daughter in school. They enlarged their gardens on the mountain slopes, and her mom and sister baked delicious buns. Then, very early in the morning, laden with pineapples, bananas, sweet potatoes, cabbages, broccoli, potatoes, and their homemade buns, they walked along the muddy path to the market in Ukarumpa Center. Once there, they spread a blanket on the ground and arranged their wares. That done, they sat down and took out their handwork. They, as most women on the market, were working on making bilum, a kind of shopping bag, which they sold at the market as well.

The Lord provides
Soon the market was swarming with people, white people from the Center as well as nationals, who came to do their shopping. When market time

was over, around 8 o'clock in the morning, all of Buddy's parents' goods were sold.

The vendors on either side of them wondered aloud, "Are your vegetables and buns better than ours? Why do all the people buy from you?" Buddy's parents just smiled; they knew that the Lord was providing for their daughter! They went to market five times a week and often sold all they had to offer. When Buddy came home from Bible School and learned what her family was doing for her and how the Lord was helping them, her heart overflowed with thankfulness to her faithful Savior.

Teaching the women of Ukarumpa

After four years of study, Buddy graduated from the Bible School. Her great desire was still to bring the gospel to her own people. Though some people attended one church or another, the majority of the nationals continued in the darkness of spirit worship.

Buddy thought, "This has to change! I want to teach the women to read and write. I want them to learn Bible texts so that they can teach their children, too." Buddy started her classes. The work progressed slowly.

Fruit on Buddy's work

One day, a boy named Tamul came home with a bloody nose. He ran to his mother and cried, "Oh, Mamma! Sauma has beaten me up so badly! I hate him!" The mother was very upset that Sauma had hurt her child. That bad boy was always tormenting her Tamul! After some minutes, however, she brightened, for now that Sauma had harmed her boy, she could demand money for payment! But then, the Bible texts she had been learning that week came into this mother's mind. She had repeated them often as she worked in the garden. "Dearly beloved, avenge not yourselves, but rather give place unto wrath: for it is written, Vengeance is mine: I will repay, saith the Lord" (Romans 12:19) and: "But I say unto you, Love your enemies, bless them that curse you, do good to them that hate you, and pray for them which despitefully use you, and persecute you" (Matthew 5:44).

She prayed silently: "Oh God, help me to do what is right!" Peace entered her heart when she said to her son, "Tamul, come, I'll clean you up, but we'll take no revenge, for God says: 'Vengeance is mine!'" Tamul looked surprised. He was not accustomed to his mother saying things like that. But the next day, he understood. As Sauma was coming down the mountain trail, a gust of wind threw him to the ground. Blood was coming from his nose. How it hurt! He felt his nose with his hand. It was broken! When Tamul and his mother heard about it, they saw that God had avenged them just like the Bible says. They also understood the meaning of the other text: "Love your enemies...." Together Tamul and his mom went to Sauma's house to ask how he was doing. They offered his family a gift of the best sweet potatoes from their garden. Tamul and Sauma shook hands, and from then on, they were best friends.

When Buddy heard this story she knew that the Lord was blessing her work indeed.

Sell all that you have

Buddy was sitting in an easy chair in her house, softly singing along with the music coming from her brand-new CD player, holding the letter she had just received from her friend. Ruth wanted to study at the university and that costs money. She needed a loan from the bank, but she had to show the bank that she could pay some of the money herself. Ruth had no money, so Buddy had emptied her own bank account to help her friend. Did Ruth write this letter to tell her how thankful she was that now she would be able to attend the university? What bitter disappointment: Ruth wrote that the bank was not satisfied with the amount Buddy had sent her. How frustrating! Ruth was so gifted. She would be able to serve the Lord much better if she had an education. Upon reading this bad news, Buddy was very sad. She wished she had more money, but her account was empty.

That night, Buddy could not sleep. Before going to bed, she had read the words, "Go and sell all that thou hast, and give to the poor, and thou shalt have treasure in heaven: and come and follow me" (Matthew 20:21). There was a great struggle in Buddy's heart. She asked God, "Do I really have to sell all, Lord? My dishes, my stove, my pots and pans, chairs, table, bed, blankets, even my new CD player?" Again the text came with power into her heart: "Sell all that you have!"

Buddy sank to her knees. With tears, she confessed that she had been too attached to earthly things. "I'll obey, Lord," she whispered.

Obedient

The next morning, in obedience to the Lord, Buddy dragged her bed, table, and chairs outside and placed all her household items on them. Great peace filled her heart as she went about this task. Customers came in droves, and soon everything was sold.

Buddy returned to her now-empty home. On the floor, she counted the money she had received that morning. There was just enough to cover her friend's university fees!

The Lord is trustworthy

That afternoon, Buddy received notice that a group of evangelists would come and have a meal at her place. How was she going to feed them, Buddy wondered. She had nothing!

The telephone rang. "Buddy, are you in need of vegetables?" "Oh, please, yes, my garden didn't do very well this season."

The phone rang again. "Buddy, I feel you need help making a meal; I will bring my staff along!"

The next morning, a man brought some chickens, and a woman a big piece of beef. And when Buddy returned from visiting a needy family, she discovered a big box on her living room floor. Inside were her own dishes, pots and pans, and cutlery, plus a good sum of money! The buyer had felt he had to return her stuff.

When the guests arrived and embraced Buddy in greeting, one after the other gave her some money. It was the Lord who moved them to give. When an envelope with 500 Kinas from an unknown giver was delivered to her house the next day, Buddy realized in deep amazement that the Lord had returned to her the full amount she had laid out for her friend's university fees.

Buddy would never forget this event. How trustworthy the Lord is!

Today

At present, Buddy is about forty years old and active in the service of the Lord. Some of her activities include directing and teaching national evangelists and working among her own people. "If you wish to teach others," she points out, "you have to know the Lord personally; otherwise there is no power in your words." May God continue to bless Buddy and her work for the extension of His kingdom!

—30—
A Christian Lady

Six days thou shalt work, but on the seventh day thou shalt rest.
—Exodus 34:21a

A young lady, named Deborah, was on her way to a southern plantation to begin her new job as a teacher. The plantation was a hundred miles away. Mr. Ramsey, the owner of the plantation, had come with several servants to meet her and accompany her home. They traveled pleasantly on through the luxuriant forests until night came on. The servants prepared a delicious meal, set up the tents for the night, and made sure Deborah had everything she needed.

The next morning was the Sabbath, the day of rest, but to her surprise, Deborah saw that Mr. Ramsey was preparing to travel further. What should she do? He was her new boss. Should she disobey him? They were in the middle of the forest —would he leave her behind if she refused to go with him? It was easy to see that beneath his gentlemanly bearing lay a haughty spirit.

Deborah knew what she had to do. She asked

A Christian Lady

the Lord for strength. Even though she was scared, she wanted to obey God, and to leave the results with Him who rules over all.

"Mr. Ramsey," began Deborah, "do you realize that today is the Lord's Day?"

"Yes, I do," answered Mr. Ramsey. "But we have a long way to go, and I'd rather not waste a perfectly good traveling day sitting in the forest."

"I'm sorry, sir, but I cannot travel today," stated Deborah.

Irritated, Mr. Ramsey responded, "Well then, it seems I'll be going on without you."

"I am not afraid to travel alone," answered Deborah, "but I *am* afraid to break God's law. I will stay here until tomorrow, and then I'll continue."

The firmness of her answer struck Mr. Ramsey. He told a friend years later, "From that moment I felt a genuine respect for Deborah. I was sure that anyone who could remain so firm in her religious convictions would also remain trustworthy in other matters."

They did not travel that Sabbath day. They rested, and continued on Monday. Deborah became the teacher of Mr. Ramsey's children. They also grew to love and respect her. Mr. Ramsey also entrusted her with other important tasks on the plantation.

We must also remain firm in obeying God. If all Christians would remain firm, even the world would respect them. Obeying God is not always

easy. Sometimes the result is pain and suffering. But Jesus said, "If a man love me, he will keep my words: and my Father will love him, and we will come unto him, and make our abode with him" (John 14:23).

—31—
Forgive us our Debts

Forbearing one another, and forgiving one another, if any man have a quarrel against any: even as Christ forgave you, so also do ye.   —Colossians 3:13

Two boys were playing together late one afternoon. All was well until Paul and Martin began to argue. They spoke very harshly to one another, using hurtful words, and parted in great anger.

When Paul got home, he went to his room and sat by the window, looking toward the west. He was feeling very unhappy as he thought about the quar-

rel he had just had with his best friend. He stared sadly out the window, watching the sun set. Suddenly these words came to his mind, "Let not the sun go down upon your wrath" (Ephesians 4:26b).

The words startled him. "I can't stand this any longer," he said to himself. He stood up and left the room, telling his mother he'd be back in a few minutes. Paul crossed the street and rang Martin's doorbell. Martin answered the door, looking very angry. But Paul said quietly, "Martin, the sun is going down, and you know the Bible says we must not let the sun go down upon our wrath. I'm sorry for arguing with you, and for saying those mean things."

Martin looked surprised, but soon a smile lit up his face. "That's okay, Paul. I'm sorry, too. You forgive me, and I'll forgive you, and we'll be friends again."

All of us can learn a lesson from this story, can we not? It is so easy to tell ourselves we did nothing wrong and that the fault is all with the other person. Sometimes it is so hard to say, "I'm sorry," isn't it? Ask the Holy Spirit to teach you true humility and true sorrow for sin.

—32—
Time Spent Wisely

Let your light so shine before men, that they may see your good works, and glorify your Father which is in heaven.
—Matthew 5:16

Three women in Westminster, England, once asked a rich man, whom we will name Mr. Johnson, to join a Bible association and help put the Bible into the hands of as many people as possible, especially those who could not afford to buy one. Mr. Johnson, however, refused, saying he believed that the Bible was a book written by the priests to deceive the people. Although he could have given money for hundreds of Bibles to be distributed, he believed the Bible was a book of lies. When the women asked his wife, she also declined, telling them she must not go against her husband's wishes.

About three months later, the same women knocked again on the Johnsons' door. Though they were polite, the man and his wife again refused.

"Would you mind if we spoke to your staff?" the women asked.

"No, I wouldn't mind at all," answered Mr. Johnson. "I don't care what they do with their money."

Mrs. Johnson led the women into the kitchen and introduced them to the people who worked for them. The visiting women explained the importance of joining a Bible association, encouraging them with stories of how the Lord had blessed their work.

"Joining the association does not cost much," the women said, "but every penny helps. The Lord can bless the smallest contribution. If you join our association, we will also make sure you have a Bible of your own if you don't already own one."

Among the servants was a young woman named Jane, who gladly joined the association. She seemed pleased with her new Bible and promised the women that she would faithfully read it. Over the next few weeks, Jane's employer noticed a change. Jane used to be a fairly good servant, but seemed to care only about herself. Now, however, she seemed to be kinder, and took care to do her job well, taking no shortcuts, and helping others if she happened to finish her tasks first.

About a half year later, Jane broke her leg, and had to be taken to a hospital to have it set. When she returned to her employer's home (for that is where she lived), everyone was very kind to her and did what they could to make her comfortable while her leg healed. Jane was very grateful that she was able to keep her job; she knew that not everyone was so blessed to have such a kind employer!

Time Spent Wisely 119

The Sunday after the doctor removed her cast, she asked if she could go out for a couple of hours.

"Certainly, Jane," smiled Mrs. Johnson. "Just be in time to help with supper."

"Yes, ma'am, I will. Thank you!" promised Jane.

Every Sunday, Jane made the same request, and after several weeks, Mrs. Johnson began to wonder where she went. She knew that whatever Jane was doing was pleasant, because she always returned with a glow of hapiness. Mrs. Johnson was too proud to ask Jane, since wealthy women should not care what their servants did on their own time, but she was actually a little jealous of Jane's happiness. Finally, the woman became so curious that she ordered her coachman, James, to follow Jane.

James followed at a safe distance, slowly travel-

ing toward the city. Sitting inside the coach, Mrs. Johnson watched in surprise as Jane entered the hospital where her broken leg had been set. Why would she want to go back there? Did she need more treatment? She certainly didn't seem to have any pain in her leg.

"What should I do, ma'am?" asked James politely.

"We'll follow her and see what she's up to. But make sure that she doesn't see us!" ordered the woman.

"Yes, ma'am!" James answered. He helped Mrs. Johnson from the coach, and then escorted her up the hospital steps. They did not hurry, but kept at a distance so that Jane would not notice them. They watched as Jane turned down one of the hallways, then entered one of the women's wards. It was a large room with beds lining the walls. Most of the beds were filled, but some were empty. At the far end of the room, a few women sat around one of the beds. Among the women was Jane with a Bible in her hands. The women were paying such close attention to what Jane was reading that no one noticed James and Mrs. Johnson. The room was very quiet, so Mrs. Johnson heard every word Jane said. The Bible reading ended, and Jane got down on her knees and began to pray. It was a simple prayer, asking God to bless His own Word and to restore the health of the patients around her.

Time Spent Wisely 121

Before Jane was finished, Mrs. Johnson whispered to James that it was time to go. She had much to think about on the ride home. What did the Bible contain, that it could change a person so much? What was so important that Jane would take her precious few hours of free time and spend it with needy strangers to tell them about this Book? Didn't the priests tell them to leave the Bible to scholars because it was much too difficult for common people to understand? Her husband was convinced the Bible was full of lies. Who was right?

After an inward struggle, Mrs. Johnson decided to ask Jane about her Bible. Seeking help from a servant was not an easy thing for a rich lady to do, but Mrs. Johnson put aside her pride. She had so many questions to ask Jane! At first, Jane was surprised, but then she gladly shared what she had learned. She explained that, at first, what she read frightened her. She realized that she was a sinner before a holy God. She did not know the Lord Jesus Christ, and without Him there is no life: "He that hath the Son hath life; and he that hath not the Son of God hath not life" (1 John 5:12). Jane explained that she read the Bible every spare moment she got, for she wanted to find the solution! Could she receive life? She read the gospels about the life of the Lord Jesus, and her heart was softened by the Holy Spirit. She began to love Him. Then she read, "Jesus said unto her, I am the resurrection, and the life: he that believeth in me, though he were dead, yet shall he live" (John 11:25). Her heart overflowed with joy, and that is why she went to share the good news of the Lord Jesus Christ with others.

Since Jane herself was just beginning to read and understand the Bible, Mrs. Johnson asked the three women from the Bible association to teach them more. It was not long before Mr. Johnson noticed a change in his wife. At first he was suspicious, and doubted that the Bible was the source of her newfound joy and peace, but then he too became interested. He had many worries in his business and worked many hours at his desk. How wonderful to be able to bring all his needs to the Lord! Before too many months had passed, the Johnsons were a completely different family. They held devotions with their servants every morning and every evening, and began attending church regularly. No longer did Mr. Johnson believe that the Bible was a book of lies. Rather, he made sure there was a Bible in every room of his house. He became a member of the committee of one of the Westminster Bible Associations.

Children, never think you are too young to serve the Lord. Jane was a young woman, employed at a lowly, simple job. Yet she set a Christ-like example, and this example made others interested in God and His Word. What do people see when they observe you? Do they want to live like you do? Do they feel you have something they don't? Do they want to attend your church because of your example? Do you reflect the Lord Jesus Christ? "The fruit of the righteous is a tree of life; and he that winneth souls is wise" (Proverbs 11:30).

—33—
Not Afraid

I will say of the LORD, He is my refuge and my fortress: my God; in him will I trust....Thou shalt not be afraid for the terror by night; nor for the arrow that flieth by day.
—Psalm 91: 2, 5

A minister visiting the island of Sicily was caught in a sudden fierce thunderstorm. He sought refuge at the first cottage he could reach to get out of the heavy rain. He was kindly welcomed by the mother of the family of four children. After introducing himself and asking several questions, the minister asked the woman if she was afraid in this terrible storm. The thunder was very loud and the lightning flashed often.

Looking up with an expression of surprise, the woman answered, "And why should I be afraid? Am I not as safe in God's protection when the thunder roars as when the sun shines brightly?"

This woman was truly happy and secure. She was strong in her faith, giving all glory to God. Every true Christian is safe in God's protection. Are you safe for this life and for eternity?

—34—
The Powder Mine

Turn not to the right hand nor to the left: remove thy foot from evil. —Proverbs 4:27

Japan and Russia had been at war, but at last it was over. The soldiers and the sailors went back to their homes, glad that there was peace again. Two years went by. One night a little town on the coast of the Sea of Japan was awakened out of its sleep by a noise that seemed to shake the earth. Trees were uprooted and houses fell in ruins. When the morning sun

rose, ten men were found dead on the shore and 156 people were injured. It seemed as if the war had begun all over again. What had happened? What had caused this death and destruction?

During the war, the sailors put powder mines out on the sea. These were explosives which floated on the water. When the big ships of the enemies struck them, they exploded, sinking the ships. One of these powder mines had obviously been floating on the waves for all this time. No ship had touched it, but at last, after two years, it touched the shore where it did its dreadful work.

Children, sin is just like that powder mine. Sometimes, people commit sin and don't seem to be punished for it. The days and weeks, and sometimes even years go by, and it seems everyone has forgotten about it. There is a verse in Numbers 32 which says, "Be sure your sin will find you out" (verse 23b). It may be that no other person knows about a particular sin which you have committed, but the Lord knows it. He says, "For mine eyes are upon all their ways: they are not hid from my face, neither is their iniquity hid from mine eyes" (Jeremiah 16:17).

The best thing to do is to flee from sin. Ask the Lord to make you hate sin. Ask Him to give you a new heart. "Depart from evil, and do good; seek peace, and pursue it" (Psalm 34:14). Does your conscience tell you that you have sinned? Do your sins trouble you? Confess your sin to God, for He can wash away all your sin. He promises, "Let the wicked forsake his way, and the unrighteous man his thoughts: and let him return unto the Lord, and he will have mercy upon him; and to our God, for he will abundantly pardon" (Isaiah 55:7).

—35—
Shaped for Heaven

That the trial of your faith, being much more precious than of gold that perisheth, though it be tried with fire, might be found unto praise and honour and glory at the appearing of Jesus Christ.
—1 Peter 1:7

I heard of a man who, during the Great Depression, lost his job, his wife, his home, and his money. He hung on tightly to the one thing he did have left — his faith. One day he stopped to watch some men doing stone work on a church. One of the workers was chiseling a triangular piece of stone.

He asked the worker, "What are you going to do with that?"

The worker replied, "See that little opening way up there near the spire? Well, I'm shaping this down here, so it will fit in up there."

As the man walked away, he realized that God had spoken through that worker to explain the ordeal he was going through: "I'm shaping you down here, so you will fit in up there."

Children, are there troubles and sorrows in your

Shaped for Heaven

young lives? What do you do with them? Do you bring them to the Lord in prayer? The Lord sends us these trials so that we may turn to Him and seek Him, not only for earthly things, but especially for the things of eternity. Do you love the Lord? If God were to take away all your earthly possessions, and your family and friends, what would you have left? Is the Lord your Savior and Redeemer? If we belong to Him, we may thank the Lord for all the "shaping" He does in our lives, because it works to bring us closer to Him.

—36—
The Wounded Soldier's Return

When Simon Peter saw it, he fell down at Jesus' knees, saying, Depart from me; for I am a sinful man, O Lord.
—Luke 5:8

One morning in 1863, a ship came to the wharf at Norfolk, Virginia, with an unusual load of passengers. The Union (or Northern) and Confederate (Southern) armies fighting in the Civil War had agreed to exchange their sick and wounded prisoners. This particular ship was bringing back several hundred Union Soldiers who had been held by the Confederates in prison hospitals. Many of these soldiers were in serious condition. There were not enough supplies and medicines to properly care for all these wounded men. Among these soldiers was a young man named Matthew, about eighteen years of age. He had been badly wounded, and was weak and sick. His time in the prison hospital, the lack of proper clothing, medicine, and food had kept him from getting well. His body was covered in painful

The Wounded Soldier's Return 131

sores, and the wounds in his leg and arm did not seem to be healing.

Matthew had received word that his elder brother William would meet him at the wharf in Norfolk and take him home to Philadelphia. But Matthew was not as happy as you would expect him to be. When he got the message, he turned sadly to his friends and sighed. "William will not know me. He won't want to have me in his nice clean home. I'll try to find a hospital, and the nurses will take care of me." Matthew wept as he looked at his filthy, ragged clothing, and his thin, sore-covered body.

As the ship touched the wharf, a strong, well-dressed man hurried up the gangplank. It was

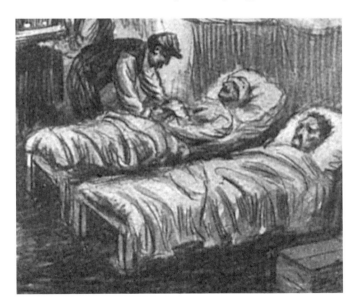

Matthew's brother, William. He had been anxiously waiting for hours. Soon he was walking past the long row of beds, looking for his sick brother. Matthew was right—William did not recognize his brother. It was not pleasant to look at the sick men. They had sores, gray faces, filthy clothes, unwashed bodies, and dirty bandages.

Matthew's heart sank. "It's just like I thought. William doesn't know me, and he'd be disgusted if he did recognize me. Look how clean and dignified he looks. He will never want someone like me in his home."

William passed by the second time and still did not recognize his brother, but Matthew did not dare to say anything. Once more, William went carefully from soldier to soldier. He had almost given up hope of finding him, fearing that perhaps Matthew had died on the way home, but he tried a third time. He stopped by Matthew's bed, still not recognizing his own brother. Gazing sadly at Matthew's pitiful condition, he whispered compassionately, "Poor fellow!" He was about to turn away, when a faint cry stopped him.

"William, don't you know me?"

In amazement, William turned and looked again at the thin figure on the bed. "My dear brother! Why didn't you say anything before?" Without waiting for an answer, William stooped and lifted his brother easily in his strong arms. He carried him,

The Wounded Soldier's Return

rags, filth, sores, and all, off the boat and into a carriage that he had waiting for him. His strength, his money, his house, his servants, and all he had were used to nurse Matthew back to health.

Children, what a beautiful picture this is of how the Lord Jesus saves His people. Jesus, the almighty, loving Savior, takes the filthy, stinking, sick, dying sinner in His arms and heals him. Just as William was happy to care for his dear brother, so Jesus loves to save sinners and make them His children. "And the Spirit and the bride say, Come. And let him that heareth say, Come. And whosoever will, let him take the water of life freely" (Revelation 22:17).

—37—
Rock of Ages

There is none holy as the LORD: for there is none beside thee: neither is there any rock like our God.
—1 Samuel 2:2

A little girl named Dora, who had learned to know and love and trust in Jesus, was visiting her friend Mary. In the living room of Mary's house hung a large picture. It showed a rock rising up in the midst of a stormy sea. On top of this rock stood a cross. Clinging to this cross was a woman who had apparently just escaped the angry waves. She seemed exhausted, but she clung closely to the rock. At her feet the artist had painted the hand of someone still in the water, grasping a part of the ship that was sinking down amidst the waves.

"Do you like the picture, Dora?" asked Mary's mother when she noticed the girl studying it.

"Yes, I do. What does it mean, though?" asked Dora.

"The painting is called The Rock of Ages," volunteered Mary.

"That's right," smiled her mother. "It is intended to represent Jesus our Savior, to whom we must cling for salvation. You know how the hymn goes:

Rock of Ages

Jesus, Lover of my soul,
Let me to Thy bosom fly,
While the raging billows roll,
While the tempest still is high.
Hide me, O my Savior, hide,
Till the storm of life is past;
Safe into the haven guide;
O receive my soul at last![1]

There's another hymn about clinging to the cross:

Nothing in my hand I bring,
Simply to Thy cross I cling;
Naked, come to Thee for dress;
Helpless, look to Thee for grace;
Foul, I to the fountain fly;
Wash me, Savior, or I die.[2]

"Oh, yes, I know those hymns," answered Dora. But after a moment's hesitation, she added, "That rock isn't really like *my* Jesus, because when I cling to Him, He reaches down and clings to me, too."

Dora had learned that her salvation did not depend on how firmly she clung to her Savior. Rather, her security was found only in Christ, who held her fast in His grip. He would never let her go, no matter how weak she might be. "In God is my salvation and my glory: the rock of my strength, and my refuge, is in God" (Psalm 62:7).

---

1. Charles Wesley (1707 - 1788).
2. Augustus Montague Toplady (1740 - 1778).

—38—
Slander and Gossip

An hypocrite with his mouth destroyeth his neighbor: but through knowledge shall the just be delivered.

—Proverbs 11:9

There was once a minister's wife who had a very effective way of stopping a person from slander or

gossip in her presence. Whenever someone would say something unpleasant about someone else, she would get her hat and coat.

"Where are you going?" the person would ask.

"I'm going to visit the person you mentioned and ask if what you said is true."

People became very cautious about speaking unkindly about anyone in her presence.

Do you participate in gossip or slandering another person? It is a very serious sin. You must fight against it and stop it completely. Ask the Lord to help you, and instead speak good things about others. Titus is directed by Paul to "put [his congregation] in mind to be subject to principalities and powers, to obey magistrates, to be ready to every good work, to speak evil of no man, to be no brawlers, but gentle, shewing all meekness unto all men" (Titus 3:1, 2).

—39—
The Bird and the Butterfly

And the Lord said, Simon, Simon, behold, Satan hath desired to have you, that he may sift you as wheat: but I have prayed for thee, that thy faith fail not.
—Luke 22: 31, 32a

A woman was taking a nap one summer afternoon while staying at the home of a friend in the country. After a while, she was awakened by a strange noise, as if something were knocking against the window.

She got out of bed to find out what it was. There, behind the curtain, on the inside of the window, was a butterfly beating frantically at the window.

The Bird and the Butterfly

What was the cause of its fear? Outside the window was a large sparrow. It sat on the outside window ledge pecking on the window, trying to get at the butterfly. The butterfly did not see the glass, nor know that it was there. But it knew that the sparrow was its enemy, and it was afraid that any minute the sparrow would eat it up. The sparrow did not see the glass either. It was expecting any minute to get hold of that tasty butterfly and eat it up.

And yet the butterfly was just as safe as if it had been miles away from that sparrow. That thick pane of glass was between it and its enemy, and that bedroom was a safe haven for it.

So it is with us when we come to Christ Jesus for refuge and abide in Him. We are perfectly safe then. His presence and His power are between us and every danger. He says to us then, as He did to Abraham, "Fear not; I am thy shield" (Genesis 15:1).

—40—
The Living God

*My soul longeth, yea, even fainteth for the courts of the L*ORD*: my heart and my flesh crieth out for the living God.*
—Psalm 84:2

At family devotions one evening, little Mary looked anxiously up at the face of her father. He was no longer living close to the Lord, and his heart had grown cold. Evening devotions were now merely form and custom, not a time of communion with God.

Mary's lips quivered as she asked, "Dad, is God dead?"

"No, my child. Why do you ask that?" responded the father.

"Well, Dad, you never talk to Him now like you used to," she replied sadly.

These words burned in the father's heart until he repented and was forgiven by his gracious heavenly Father. "The father of the righteous shall greatly rejoice: and he that begetteth a wise child shall have joy of him" (Proverbs 23:24).

—41—
Lying Worse than Stealing

These are the things that ye shall do; Speak ye every man the truth to his neighbour; execute the judgment of truth and peace in your gates.
—Zechariah 8:16

A little girl was talking with her mother at breakfast one morning. "Mommy," she asked, "what do you think is worse, lying or stealing?"

"I don't know, dear," answered her mother. "They are both sins which God forbids."

"I've been thinking," continued the little girl thoughtfully, "and I've decided that lying is worse than stealing. If you steal something, you can bring it back or pay for it, but when you tell a lie, it's there forever."

—42—
An Apology

Put them in mind...to speak evil of no man, to be no brawlers, but gentle, shewing all meekness unto all men.
—Titus 3:2

There once was a man named Mr. Douglas, who was a Christian. He had been talking to Mr. Jameson, who was not a Christian. Mr. Jameson had a bad temper. He was angry at Mr. Douglas because of something Mr. Douglas had said to him. Mr. Jameson was very surprised when Mr. Douglas knocked at his door.

An Apology

"What do you want?" he asked roughly.

"Mr. Jameson, I have come to apologize for what I said to you earlier today. I am sorry it offended you. I've come to ask for your forgiveness."

Mr. Jameson was speechless. This was not what he expected. He had been prepared to shout and scold. After a moment he said, "Of course, I forgive you, Mr. Douglas."

After Mr. Douglas had left, Mr. Jameson sat down in a chair. "What a strange man this is!" he thought to himself. "Everybody knows what a bad temper I have. It was probably not easy for him to come and apologize. He probably thought I would shout at him. But still he came to see me! I wonder if it's because he's a Christian. Maybe Christianity is a good thing after all. I'd better look into it."

And Mr. Jameson did look into it. He began to attend church services, and to read his Bible. He learned to pray. The Holy Spirit began to work in his heart, and renewed him. He learned, by God's grace, to control his temper, and to be patient and kind. "If any man among you seem to be religious, and bridleth not his tongue, but deceiveth his own heart, this man's religion is vain" (James 1:26). "He that is slow to anger is better than the mighty; and he that ruleth his spirit than he that taketh a city" (Proverbs 16:32).

—43—
The Retired Businessman

As we have therefore opportunity, let us do good unto all men, especially unto them who are of the household of faith.
—Galatians 6:10

Once there was a businessman, named Mr. Matthews, who lived in London. He had been very successful and had become very rich. He lived in a beautiful mansion in the country. When he sold his business for a large sum of money, he looked forward to his retirement. The mansion he lived in was filled with beautiful things. The halls, parlors, dining rooms, and library were filled with rare and

interesting items which he had acquired in his many travels. The floors were decorated with lovely carpets from Brussels and Turkey; the furniture was crafted by the best carpenters; and the walls were adorned with splendid mirrors and exquisite paintings. Carriages, horses, grooms, and servants were at his command. Books, pictures, and engravings were at hand to interest him. Newspapers and periodicals were brought to his table so that he could keep up with the news of the world. Friends and acquaintances came to visit and to see his lovely home.

But Mr. Matthews was not happy. He was lonely: he was not married, and had no children. He had no aim, no goal in life. Saddest of all, he was not a Christian. Nothing gave him joy. His business friends no longer came to visit. He did not enjoy reading the business section of the papers anymore because he was no longer involved in the business world. None of the news stories interested him anymore because he felt detached from the world around him. He no longer cared about politics: he had his fortune now and was trying to enjoy it, but he could find no joy or satisfaction in all the wealth surrounding him.

Soon, everything seemed worthless. The beautiful rooms in his mansion were unused; his horse and carriage stood idle in the barn; his books went unread, his newspapers untouched. He did not even enjoy his beautifully prepared meals anymore.

Mr. Matthews lost all interest in life. He wanted to commit suicide. No one would miss him anyway, he thought dejectedly.

Saturday night arrived, and he decided that before dawn the next morning, before people awoke, he would make his way to the Waterloo Bridge and jump into the river. At three o'clock in the morning, he started on his tragic journey. He had nearly reached the bridge when he noticed a person standing at the railing. Cautiously, Mr. Matthews tried to pass without drawing attention to himself. The last thing he wanted was someone witnessing his last moments. However, he couldn't help stopping when he saw the poor, miserable, tattered man in front of him.

"What are you doing here?" inquired Mr. Matthews.

The man turned to look at him. Mr. Matthews thought he had never seen a sadder face. "I have a wife and family, sir," replied the man. "I don't dare to go back to them. They are starving and we are to be evicted[1] today. I have nothing to offer my family anymore, and I simply can't face them."

The businessman felt sorry for the man. He put his hand into his pocket and took out some money. "Here. This will be of more use to you than to me."

---

1. To be evicted means to be put out of your home because you didn't pay the rent.

"Oh, thank you, sir!" exclaimed the man, hardly believing what he saw in his hands. "God bless you, sir! God bless you!" The man was so overcome that he knelt in the street in front of Mr. Matthews.

"Stop!" said Mr. Matthews, embarrassed. He couldn't believe that what he thought to be such a small amount of money could mean so much to someone. "Tell me where you live. And what is your name?"

"I live in Lambeth, sir, and my name is John Andrews."

"Then why are you here this morning?"

"I don't really want to admit it," replied Mr. Andrews, hanging his head. "I am ashamed of myself."

"Why?"

"Well, sir, I didn't have any money, and I have no job although I've tried hard to find work. I came here to drown myself even though I knew it was wrong."

The businessman was surprised but said nothing. After a long silence, he said, "Mr. Andrews, I am a rich man, and yet I am so miserable that I came here this morning for the same reason you did. I think there is a reason we met. Let me go with you to meet your family."

Mr. Andrews made every excuse he could think of to prevent Mr. Matthews from meeting his family, but the businessman was determined.

"Have you committed any crimes?" asked Mr. Matthews as they walked along the dark streets. He knew that many poor people were driven to steal out of desperation.

"No, sir, we have tried to make ends meet by earning money however we could, but we are so miserably poor. For all I know, my wife and children may be out on the street right now."

"Why is it that you cannot find any work?"

"I used to groom the horses of the stage coaches," answered Mr. Andrews, "but since the railroads have been built, stage coaches are not used much anymore, and many men like myself are unemployed."

Together, Mr. Andrews and Mr. Matthews walked the two miles to the poor man's home. At last they approached an old, dilapidated building.

The Retired Businessman

Suddenly, a woman opened the door. As soon as she saw Mr. Andrews, she began to scold him, demanding an explanation for his long absence in the middle of the night. Obviously, she had been very worried. But when her husband placed the money he had just received from Mr. Matthews into her hand, she became quiet. Staring in surprise at the wealthy man, as though noticing him for the first time, she politely asked him to come inside. Mr. Matthews had never associated with poor people before, since his business involved contacts only with the rich. He asked the Andrews many questions, and soon decided that the main problem in this family was lack of money. He was shocked at the ragged looking children, but was happy to see their good manners. Mr. and Mrs. Andrews did love each other and their children, but were sad and frustrated at being unable to provide enough food and clothing for the family.

Using her meager supplies, Mrs. Andrews made breakfast, and Mr. Matthews told the family his plan. He promised them that better days lay ahead for all of them. After breakfast, Mr. Matthews returned home, taking Mr. Andrews with him. With his own hands, Mr. Matthews helped load a cart with food, clothing, bedding, and furniture for the needy family. Mr. Andrews left after thanking the rich man profusely.

After the poor man had gone, Mr. Matthews was

left alone to think about the strange events of the morning. He felt much better after having helped the poor, starving family. Out of mere selfishness, he decided that doing good for others would make him happier. He did not make this decision out of love to God or thankfulness for all the blessings God had showered him with, but only because it made him feel good inside. He gave Mr. Andrews a job at his stables, and found a nicer home for the Andrews family, very near his own home. The children were able to attend school. This made Mr. Matthews feel much better. Once again, he felt a reason to get up in the morning, knowing people needed him.

Soon he sought out other poor families to help. God, however, did not leave Mr. Matthews after preventing him from committing suicide. It was God who had arranged for Mr. Matthews and Mr. Andrews to meet at the bridge that dark Sunday morning. The Lord's greatest work, however, is the salvation of sinners for the glory of His great Name. This is just what He did for Mr. Matthews. Through the work of the Holy Spirit and conversations with these poor families, Mr. Matthews discovered the cause of all his misery. He saw that it was his sin that made him miserable. He had lived his whole life only for himself. True, he was now helping others, and this gave him some satisfaction. But he needed more. Mr. Matthews met some of God's people who were very poor, yet very happy. At first he could not understand it, but then the Holy Spirit taught him the source of their joy. They had lain "up for [themselves] treasures in heaven, where neither moth nor rust doth corrupt, and where thieves do not break through nor steal" (Matthew 6:20). These poor people had not built their foundation on the sandy foundation of this world, but on the Rock, the Lord Jesus Christ. Mr. Matthews was led to the Savior, and then, finally, Mr. Matthews found true happiness.

Now he had a goal in life. He helped poor families with their physical needs, but his greatest joy was to help them with their spiritual needs. His wealth was used in God's service, and his work among the poor was greatly blessed by the Lord. Many people were helped by this kind man, and relieved of their earthly needs, but God was also pleased to bless the efforts of Mr. Matthews to guide people to the true source of happiness. With tears, he often told his story, how the Lord sent Mr. Andrews to him to stop him from drowning himself. How happy he was to be used by the Lord in His service! "For what is a man profited, if he shall gain the whole world, and lose his own soul? or what shall a man give in exchange for his soul?" (Matthew 16:19).

BUILDING ON THE ROCK
Daily Devotional Stories for Children
By Joel R. Beeke and Diana Kleyn

Vol. 1 – How God Used a Thunderstorm
Themes: Virtuous Living and the Value of Scripture
ISBN 1-85792-815-6   Paperback, 145 pages

Vol. 2 – How God Stopped the Pirates
Themes: Missionary Tales and Remarkable Conversions
ISBN 1-85792-816-4   Paperback, 163 pages

Vol. 3 – How God Used a Snowdrift
Themes: Honoring God and Dramatic Deliverances
ISBN 1-85792-817-2   Paperback, 171 pages

Vol. 4 – How God Used a Drought and an Umbrella
Themes: Faithful Witnesses and Childhood Faith
ISBN 1-85792-818-0   Paperback, 162 pages

Vol. 5 – How God Sent a Dog to Save a Family
Themes: God's Care and Childhood Faith
ISBN 1-85792-819-9   Paperback, 165 pages

REFORMATION HERITAGE BOOKS
2965 Leonard St., NE, Grand Rapids, MI 49525
www.heritagebooks.org or orders@heritagebooks.org
(616) 977-0599